Scandinavian Development Agreements with African Countries

SCANDINAVIAN DEVELOPMENT AGREEMENTS WITH AFRICAN COUNTRIES

Carl Gösta Widstrand
Zdenek Červenka

The Scandinavian Institute of African Studies
Uppsala 1971

Litho by Kå-We Tryck, Uppsala.
Printed by Uppsala Offset Center AB.
Uppsala 1971.
ISBN 91-7106-050-2

CONTENTS

PREFACE   7
INTRODUCTION   9
   Economic-development agreements between Scandinavian and
   African countries   9
I. POLICY ON DEVELOPMENT AID IN THE SCANDINAVIAN
   COUNTRIES   13
   The scope and volume of the development aid in general   14
   The channels of development assistance   16
   The selection of African recipients of development assistance   18
   Joint Nordic projects   22
II. THE MACHINERY FOR THE ADMINISTRATION OF
   DEVELOPMENT AID   24
   Sweden   24
   Denmark   25
   Finland   26
   Norway   27
III. TYPES OF DEVELOPMENT AGREEMENTS   29
   Agreements of a general character   30
   Agreements concerning a specific programme or project   30
   Joint agreements between several donors and one recipient   31
IV. THE GENERAL TERMS AND CONDITIONS UNDER WHICH
   SCANDINAVIAN FINANCIAL AID IS PROVIDED   33
   The problem of the tying of aid   33
V. THE NATURE OF THE OBLIGATIONS OF THE CONTRACT-
   ING PARTIES TO THE DEVELOPMENT AGREEMENT   37
VI. STATUS OF THE PERSONNEL PROVIDED UNDER
   DEVELOPMENT AGREEMENTS   40
   Tax and customs exemption and other privileges   41
   Immunity from legal proceedings etc.   42
   The status of the Scandinavian personnel compared with that
   of other countries   44

VII. THE SETTLEMENT OF DISPUTES   47
VIII. CONCLUSIONS   49
NOTES   53
ANNEX I: Seven points of Swedish foreign aid policy
          by Ernst Michanek, Director-General, SIDA   64
ANNEX II: Basic plan for Swedish official development assistance,
          1969/70 - 1972/73   69
ANNEX III: Norwegian net official development assistance   70
ANNEX IV: Danish development assistance 1962 - 70   71
ANNEX V: Flow of Finnish resources to less-developed countries
          and multilateral agencies   72
ANNEX VI: Organisation chart of the Swedish International
          Development Authority (SIDA)   73
ANNEX VII: Organisation chart of the Norwegian Agency for
          International Development (NORAD)   74

PREFACE

This study was presented in draft form to the *United Nations Regional Symposium for African Law*, held in Accra, Ghana, in January 1971. Copies of the draft were sent to the Scandinavian assistance agencies: the Danish International Development Authority (DANIDA), the Norwegian Agency for International Development (NORAD), the Bureau of Technical Assistance of the Finnish Foreign Ministry and the Swedish International Development Authority (SIDA). Corrections and additions have been incorporated in this text, which also includes a summary of the discussions at the Accra Conference, where the Institute was represented by Dr. Zdenek Červenka.

While national programmes are given considerable publicity in the information issued by the various departments, this is the first attempt to give information on the development efforts made by the Scandinavian countries, to try to assess and compare some of their features and to explain the machinery for their implementation. We are convinced that serious programmes of assistance and aid must have broad, national, popular support, not only because the taxpayers provide the bulk of the funds available and therefore are entitled to know what happens to their contributions, but also because it is necessary to create a firm, positive attitude to aid. This must be done by appealing less to feeling and more to reason and to fact. One of the amins of the Scandinavian Institute of African Studies at Uppsala is to provide this type of information, both in Scandinavia and abroad.

For helpful criticism and comments, the authors would like to thank especially Mr. Tor Kvarnbäck, of the SIDA, Messrs. V. Christiansen, Hans Jespersen and Jörgen Milwertz, of the DANIDA, Mrs. Eldfrid Bjørdal, of the NORAD, and Miss Ritva Alanaatu and Mr. Jaakko Iloniemi, of the Bureau of Technical Assistance of the Finnish Foreign Ministry.

C.G. Widstrand
Zdenek Červenka

Uppsala, March 1971

INTRODUCTION

Economic-development agreements between Scandinavian and African countries

The various aspects of economic-development agreements were one of the topics of the United Nations Regional Symposium for African Law, organized by the United Nations Institute for Training and Research (UNITAR) and held in January 1971 in Accra, Ghana.

The other two topics were "State Succession on Matters Other than Treaties" and "The Historical Contribution of Africa to International Law". The objective of the symposium was described as "to foster the role of international law as a means of promoting the purposes of the United Nations, assisting the development of international co-operation at regional and universal levels and facilitating the solution of problems confronting the states in their mutual relations".

Six days were spent discussing the economic-development agreements and the discussion was based on four major papers. The first was prepared by Dr. O.L. Adegbite, of the Faculty of Law at the University of Lagos, and was entitled "The Legal Framework of Development Agreements in Africa". The second was written by Mr. A.M. Akiwumi, the Regional Adviser on Economic Co-operation of the U.N. Economic Commission for Africa, and was entitled "A Legal Profile of Economic Co-operation in East Africa 1947-67". The third was a "Functional Analysis of the Economic Development Agreements", prepared by Tom J. Farer, of Columbia University, New York. The last was written by Dr. Z. Cervenka and Professor C.G. Widstrand, of the Scandinavian Institute of African Studies in Uppsala, and was concerned with "The Pattern of the Development Agreements between the Scandinavian and the African Countries", a subject which occupies the major part of the present paper.

It was rather significant that development agreements were understood by the majority of the participants to be agreements which embody the terms under which private (or state) capital is invited into a developing country and the terms on which it is offered. The characteristics of such agreements have been described by Lord McNair as follows:

(1) They are made between a government, on the one side, and a foreign corporation, on the other.

(2) They usually provide for some long-term exploitation of natural resources, involving permanent installations and long-term relationships.

(3) They often involve the creation of rights which are not purely contractual but more akin to property rights, such as the possession of parts of the territory of the contracting state.

(4) They involve the vesting in the foreign corporation of certain rights of a semi-political character, with certain privileges, such as tax exemptions, on the one side, and certain special responsibilities for the maintenance of order and security, on the other.

(5) These agreements are governed in part by public and in part by private law.

(6) Their insertion and execution very often involve the protection of the state to whose laws the corporation owes its existence.

(7) There is often little in common between the legal system of the host country and that of the mother country of the investing corporation.

(8) There is frequently reference to arbitration in the case of disputes – arbitration, which excludes the jurisdiction of the national courts of both parties.[1]

Apart from the questions whether the agreement should incorporate an explicit measure of compensation in case of nationalization and what guarantees the host country can offer to the foreign investors, a wider problem, namely, "What qualifications are expected from the country to which the capital is supplied?", was discussed at great length.

Contrary to the general belief, the question of guarantees (of non-nationalization, non-expropriation, adequate compensation, etc.) is not really a decisive factor in the foreign investor's policy-making. One of the participants offered evidence that the existence and availability of investment guarantees actually plays a marginal role in the investment decision-making process. As Professor A.A. Fatouros, of Indiana University, put it: "It is never a controlling factor, it may at best be a favourable consideration, taken into view at the last stage of the process, when the form and manner of the investment, and no longer its desirability, are being studied. While it is highly unlikely that the availability of investment guarantees has ever induced an investment, their absence may in some marginal cases have affected negatively the undertaking of an investment." Indeed, the qualification of the country for foreign investment does not really depend on the existence of guarantees in the form of legal norms but on *the prospect of the stability of the government and in its practical policies towards the investors.*

Dr. Adegbite pointed out in his paper that

... foreign Governments and private investors are, on the other hand, very much aggrieved at the growing insecurity of foreign investments in Africa. It is true that, while a number of countries have promulgated statutes which aim at strengthening the protection of foreign investments,[2] many have gone further to provide for incentives to investors in the form of tax relief and lesser restraints on repatriation of capital and profit. At the same time many African states have polluted the investment atmosphere with their cavalier resort to nationalisation of foreign assets in a manner which smacks of confiscation.

This statement provoked a great many critical remarks. Participants from Algeria, Kenya, Tanzania and Zambia felt that African governments are justified in seeking better terms either than those inherited from the colonial past or when the circumstances under which the agreements were concluded had considerably changed.

The African political scene, with many and unexpected political changes and *coups d'état* has a two-fold effect on the investors' policy decisions:

(1) It reduces the numbers of countries "eligible" for investment and

(2) It leads to the kind of short-term ventures in which capital and profit are repatriated in the quickest possible way.

As many of the political upheavals are caused or triggered off by the deterioration of a country's economy, one of the aspects of achieving political stability is considered to be long-term investments. Such investments are not made in "unstable" countries, foreign capital does not flow into such countries, and the number of countries eligible decreases every day. Precisely for this reason, countries like Tanzania are trying to solve this problem by a policy of self-reliance and by trying to rely on a mass mobilization of resources rather than on foreign investments.

This fundamental question – the question whether foreign investment is an essential condition of development – was raised at the outset of the discussion in Accra. Dr. T. Kunugi, of the United Nations Secretariat in New York, wondered whether it was not at least conceivable that development could be achieved through a rigorous programme of self-reliance, and he quoted the example of Japan.

But there appeared to be almost unanimous rejection of this proposition. The example of Japan was different on several grounds: the internal market provided by Japan's large and concentrated population; the powerful administrative mechanism available to the state for purposes of capital mobilisation; and the severe burden imposed on the agricultural sector of Japanese society, the implication being that equivalent burdens either could not or should not be imposed in contemporary Africa. The need for private foreign investment was also attributed to the serious and growing technology gap and to the failure of the economically developed states to provide financial assistance in sufficient quantities or at sufficiently low rates of interest to avoid a crushing debt-repayment burden. What emerged from the conference was the recognition of the fact that, even if the main responsibility for their future progress lies in the hands of the countries themselves, the actual pace of development will depend on the assistance given to them by the industrial countries and on the ways in which this assistance is given.

This is also reflected in the development agreements, which are the instruments by which this assistance is given. They fall mainly into two categories:

(1) Agreements concluded between the foreign investors (private or government-sponsored) and the government, corporation (state or private) of the developing country. While these agreements do promote the development of the recipient country, they are concluded strictly on a commercial basis and on commercial considerations. The motivation of the foreign investors is to make profits. The question of development needs is of secondary importance (if any), though, of course, lip service is paid to it.

(2) Agreements, the object of which is to provide aid by means of technical assistance, credits and loans. Needless to say, the scope of these agreements varies considerably. They range from the agreements providing for "tied aid" to the agreements actually meeting the requirements of a developing country.[3]

We hold the view that the term "development agreement" is justified only in cases of agreements in which the aim is actually and genuinely to promote development and not business interests.[4]

This category of development agreements has, however, some interesting aspects, and a substantial part of this paper is concerned with an analysis of the agreements of this type concluded between Scandinavian[5] and African countries.

I. POLICY ON DEVELOPMENT AID IN THE SCANDINAVIAN COUNTRIES

The fundamental question concerning any country's decision to give aid is that of the motives behind it. At one of the first conferences concerned with aid to developing countries in Milan in 1954, the then leader of the British Labour Party, the late Hugh Caitskell, summed up the debate on the reasons for giving aid in the following words:

> Just as, within countries, we now accept it that we should tax the rich to help the poor, so, between countries, it is the moral duty of the rich to help the poor. I think basically it is only on the moral precept that it is right for those who have not that we must rely for the justification of aid.[6]

In his address to the Commonwealth Conference in Singapore in 1971, the Prime Minister of Ghana, Dr. Kofi Busia, commented on Gaitskell's words thus:

> To me, it marks an advance in the moral consciousness of the world, and in the moral content of the concept of world community. It is in accord with the increasing interdependence of nations made possible, and also compelled by contemporary science and technology, and the patterns of trade and the prerequisites for further economic growth.[6]

The Scandinavian efforts in this respect may be ascribed to a large extent to feelings of moral duty and international solidarity. The claims to social equality that have marked the development of our countries during the past century are no longer of an exclusively national concern but something increasingly universal and international. The idealistic motives behind the assistance are thus at the same time highly realistic and there is in many respects a strong correlation between the policy at home, defined in terms of social justice, social security and free education for all at all levels, and the foreign policy towards the developing countries. This policy has its origin in the firm belief that a subscription to the basic principles of human rights — freedom, equality and the right of self-determination — is meaningless unless it is linked with material assistance to achieve or help their implementation.

The present policy on aid and technical assistance in the Scandinavian countries is a follow-up of their participation in the United Nations Technical Assistance Programme launched in 1948 and in its second phase, the Expanded Programme of Technical Assistance (EPTA) of 1949.

The scope and volume of the development aid in general

The first *Swedish* bilateral programme dates from 1952, when the Central Committee for Swedish Technical Assistance to Less Developed Countries came into existence. Its first practical result was an agreement in 1954 between Sweden and Ethiopia concerning assistance to the Ethio-Swedish Institute of Building Technology. Up to 1961, Swedish aid totalled $23.2 million. The year 1962, when Government Bill No. 100 was adopted, saw the assistance given to the developing countries increased to $25.1 million.[7] Six years later a new Bill[8] was adopted by the Swedish Parliament, providing for a considerable expansion of official assistance. According to this Bill, the official budgetary appropriations for development assistance will reach 1 per cent of the GNP in the fiscal year 1974-75. Budgetary appropriations for loans are the amounts made available by the Swedish Parliament which represent the Swedish commitments in the forthcoming financial year. As regards the grants or technical assistance, the appropriations by the Parliament represent the actual disbursements. Sometimes this amount is not fully utilized for various reasons. For example, the preparation of the project under consideration may not have been completed in time and the discursement may thus have been delayed. The amount which is actually transferred to the recipient countries during the current financial year is called the "net flow". In 1969 the net flow of Swedish official development assistance reached the level of $120 million, which represents an increase of 69 per cent from the 1968 level of $71 million. The official development assistance, expressed as a percentage of the GNP, was 0.43 per cent in 1969. The total flow, including both the official and private resources, amounted to 0.75 per cent, compared with 0.49 per cent in 1968. If contributions from the private non-profit-making organisations are included, the total flow amounts to 0.81 per cent of the GNP. Between 1967 and 1968 the corresponding increase was 19 per cent. The 1970 figures of disbursements of Swedish official assistance, which have not yet been released, are believed to reach *c.* $140 millions (see also Annex II).

Norway's first bilateral programme also dates from 1952, when an agreement was concluded with the Indian Government providing for Norwegian assistance in the development of fisheries and the fish-processing industry in south-western India. Since 1952, Norway's appropriations for development assistance have steadily increased and in 1969, in accordance with the medium-term plan for achieving official appropriations representing 0.75 per cent of the gross national project by 1974, reached the sum of $29.7 million, an increase of about 8 per cent above 1968.

Due to the extraordinarily high level of the assistance given to Nigeria in 1968, the percentage increase was not as high as during the last few years. Appropriations for development assistance in 1970 amounted to $36.7 million, as compared with $29.7 million in 1969. Private transfers remained relatively high in 1969, reaching more than $37 million. The greater part of this flow was in the form of export credits to countries on the DAC list of developing countries. Investments, however, increased by about 150 per cent, compared with 1968, and amounted to approximately $11 million. In total, net Norwegian transfers thus increased from $57.7 million in 1968 to 75.2 million dollars in 1969. (For a survey of the Norwegian net development assistance, see Annex III.)

In 1969 *Danish* disbursements for official development assistance totalled $54.3 million, corresponding to 0.40 per cent of the GNP (at market prices), which for 1969 is provisionally estimated at $13.8 billion. The item "other official flows" was $0.5 million, representing equity investments by the Industrialization Fund for Developing Countries. Guaranteed private export credits, which usually account for the bulk of these flows, amounted to $84.7 million net, corresponding to 0.61 per cent of the GNP. Compared with 1968, official development assistance increased by $25.6 million, or 89 per cent. From 1967 to 1968 the growth rate was only about 10 per cent. The reason was that the utilization of appropriations was unevenly distributed over the fiscal year, with a very heavy concentration of disbursements in the first quarter of 1969. (For a survey of Denmark's development assistance for the years 1962-70 and estimates for 1971-3, see Annex IV).

The total flow of *Finland's* official development assistance in 1969 reached $9,647,217, more than three times the amount ($2,974,583) in 1968. During the 25th commemorative session of the U.N. General Assembly, Finland subscribed to the objectives and goals spelt out in he International Development Strategy. This implied, among other things, that the Finnish Government pledged its support to the new official-aid target (0.7% of the gross national product) to be reached in the middle of the 1970's. For

Finland this means almost eight times as much in aid as has been appropriated for 1970 ($9.2 million). A considerable part of these resources will, even in the future, be channelled through multilateral programmes. The bilateral programme will consist of two main components, technical assistance and soft credits. Technical assistance will be channelled to the countries with which Finland has already concluded agreements, namely, Ethiopia, Tanzania, Tunisia, and Zambia. (For a survey of the Finnish flow of resources to less developed countries and multilateral agencies, see Annex V.)

The channels of development assistance

One of the main features of Scandinavian aid to the developing countries has always been its strong support for the international co-ordination of development assistance within the framework of the United Nations. In the case of Sweden the assistance provided on the multilateral basis in the last decade, at least up to 1968, constituted about 40 per cent of the total volume of Swedish aid, compared with the average of merely 10 per cent provided by the other western countries. The main reason for the emphasis on aid channelled through the United Nations specialized agencies rather than aid provided on a bilateral basis has been to meet the understandable preference of the recipient countries for anonymous aid, which is considerably freed from political strings.

Bilateral aid, by its very nature, implies a dependence of the recipient on the donor, which makes it difficult to conceive of the sovereign equality of the two contracting parties. The Swedish policy of promoting a concept of universality and anonymity in international development was defined in Government Bill No. 100 of 1962. This document states that Sweden finds it difficult to link assistance with any particular social or political aims. In the words of the Bill: "We must not assume that the social and political principles to which we subscribe are either practicable or desirable in all countries. In spite of this, we can reasonably try so to direct our assistance programs that they tend, in the best judgement, to promote political democracy and social equality." In the opinion of the Swedish Government, this can be better achieved by a joint international effort rather than on a bilateral basis only. It should be pointed out, however, that, while the policy of the Scandinavian countries still continues to be that of supporting international action, the actual share of assistance provided under bilateral agreements has a tendency to continuously increase.

In the case of *Sweden* the general contributions to multilateral programmes in 1969-70 amounted to nearly $61 million, while the bilateral development assistance totalled $67.6 million, with a prospect of reaching nearly $95 million in 1970-1, compared with the $54.6 million representing multilateral aid.

There has also in *Denmark* been a tendency to a faster rate of growth in bilateral than in multilateral aid, despite the official anouncement that multilateral and bilateral aid would account for roughly 50% each of the official development assistance. Considerable year-to-year fluctuations — especially due to the difficulties in forecasting disbursements under bilateral loan agreements — are unavioidable. In 1969 bilateral aid totalled $30.8 million, a rise of 94% over 1968, while multilateral aid accounted for $23.5 million, an increase of 82% over 1968. In the financial years 1968-9 and 1969-70, Denmark concluded, in all, 38 bilateral development agreements with 11 countries.

The proportion of multilateral to bilateral development assistance provided by *Norway* is more balanced than those of Sweden and Denmark. Multilateral aid, amounting to $16,121 million, still considerably exceeds the bilateral aid, totalling $13,404 million. The policy of allocating about 50 per cent of the total official appropriations to multilateral channels is likely to be continued in the future.[9]

Finland's official multilateral aid, a total of $7,879,680 in 1969, represents almost four times the amount provided under the bilateral arrangements ($1,767,527).

The decrease of the volume of multilateral aid (especially in the cases of Sweden and Denmark) should not be taken as a change of policy on the part of all Nordic countries in putting great emphasis on multilateral aid. The explanation of the rise of the bilateral programme is simply that it started later than the multilateral programme advanced by the United Nations. It is obviously a time-consuming process for countries with only a few traditional links with the Third World to build up a bilateral aid programme.

But there are other factors involved in Sweden's and Denmark's increases of bilateral aid. In Sweden one of them is the pressure from within the national agency handling the development assistance, the Swedish International Development Agency (SIDA), which prefers bilateral arrangements on the ground that they are far more effective. The view held is that uninterrupted and direct co-operation between the SIDA and the recipient country offers opportunities of rectifying any failings which may appear in the course of the implementation of an agreed project. Bilateral arrangements involving the direct presence of Sweden in a recipient country make it easier to satisfy the demands of the Swedish taxpayer, who wants to know how and where his money is being spent.

Another factor is the readiness of the African countries to enter into bilateral agreements with the Scandinavian countries on account of their non-colonial past[10] and, above all, their resolute stand on the issues of the decolonization of Africa and apartheid. In this connection it should be pointed out that Sweden and Norway are exceptional among the western countries in providing direct aid to the liberation movements in Africa. This aid is of a humanitarian character and is formally destined to the individuals in the areas concerned. From necessity, however, it has to be channelled through the various liberation movements operating in the territories. This formula makes the granting of aid compatible with Swedish neutrality. The amount of aid for this purpose amounted in 1969-70 to more than $1 million.[11]

The new role of development aid as one of the means of giving active support to those African states bordering on colonies and states pursuing a policy of apartheid was emphasized by the Swedish delegate to the United Nations, Mr. Olof Rydbeck, in explaining the joint Scandinavian policy in the Fourth Committee debate on South Africa on October 13, 1970:

> We must also recognize the importance of a general strengthening of the economic and political stability of free Africa, in particular, the need for special measures to assist those who are situated in the immediate neighbourhood of the racially oppressed territories. Our aim should be to increase their ability to resist pressure from the minority regimes in southern Africa, thereby helping to release then from undue dependence on these regimes.

The selection of African recipients of development assistance

An interesting feature of the Scandinavian development programme in

Africa is its concentration primarily on English-speaking countries and on East Africa. One explanation of this lies in the educational systems of the Scandinavian countries, where English is the first foreign language taught in the primary schools. While most other countries and in particular the former colonial powers have continued to pursue their interests in their former colonies and trading partners, Scandinavian countries have not followed their trading patterns in this respect. Denmark has long-standing trading interests in West Africa, but its aid is channelled largely to East Africa. The Norwegians have traded in stockfish for years with Nigeria, but their assistance to Nigeria is only a small percentage of the total budget. Swedish private interests have long been focused on Liberia, where the Liberian-American-Swedish Minerals Company (LAMCO) has been operating since 1955, but Swedish assistance to Liberia – a small educational project – is negligible. It is true that the Nigerian war aroused considerable emotions in all the Scandinavian countries and resulted in substantial humanitarian aid being flown and shipped to the civilian victims of the war,[1,2] but even that did not affect the priorities of the development aid, which continues to be centred on East Africa. Behind the arguments about the advantages of concentrating aid in one area rather than distributing it among several countries in such a vast continent, there may be other reasons. Since the Swedish Red Cross Ambulance Unit was sent to the Italo-Abyssinian war, Swedish interest in Ethiopia has increased, owing to the prolonged presence of Swedish missionaries in that country and the use of Swedish Air Force and Army experts to build up the Ethiopian armed forces during the forties and fifties. There has, however, been increasing criticism of the Swedish engagement in Ethiopia.

Interest in Tanzania is of tremendous proportions in Scandinavia today, in schools, in the universities and among the general public, and the activities in Tanzania have general support. This is probably due to two factors: the personality of President Nyerere and the Tanzanian policy of development through socialism, including the ideas of non-alignment and self-reliance. Scandinavians are romantics. Scandinavian ideas about the importance of poverty in national development, which allegedly makes people self-reliant, industrious and forward-looking, both in the fields and in the schools, may still underlie the romantic identification with the Tanzanian struggle.

However, Swedish interest in Tanzania back in the middle fifties was also influenced by a very small number of key persons allied with the Swedish Lutheran mission. Missionaries were almost the only people in Scandinavia with any experience of Africa, and these people were available, with their experience of an English-speaking country and their belief in Nyerere and the future of Tanganyika. This in turn influenced the choice of Tanzania for a joint Scandinavian project.

It should be mentioned, however, that the question of the selection of the countries to which aid in the form of technical assistance, credits or loans should be made available is a topic of heated public discussion.[1][3]

In terms of technical development assistance Ethiopia received $5.841 million — 18.6 per cent of the total *Swedish* development aid — in 1968-9 and is still leading with $5.802 million in 1970-1, representing 10.9 per cent of Swedish development aid. Tanzania comes second with $4.719 million, which accounts for 7.2 per cent of the total Swedish aid in 1970-1, followed closely by Kenya, which received in the same period $3.172 million (6 per cent of the total Swedish aid). The Sudan was granted a credit of $7 million in 1966 for the development of rural water supplies. A further credit of $3 million was granted for the same purpose in 1970. Development assistance to Zambia is $1.025 million, which is nearly double the amount in 1969-70 ($0.444 million), and will reach $1.625 million in 1971-2. Tunisia is the recipient of the largest portion of Swedish development assistance granted to the other than English-speaking countries. The volume of technical assistance reached $2.321 million in 1970-1, representing 4.4 per cent of the total Swedish aid. As far as credit is concerned, Tanzania tops the list of African borrowers from Sweden with $5.997 million in 1970-1, with the prospect of the sum of $10.638 million in 1971-2. The credit granted to Kenya is $2.901 million in 1970-1 and is to be more than doubled in 1971-2, when it will amount to $6.769 million. The third largest borrower is Ethiopia, with $2.224 million in the 1970-1 period. Assistance to agriculture and food production, education and family planning constitute the principal components of Swedish development aid. Algeria, Botswana, Lesotho, Morocco and Swaziland also receive Swedish aid, though on a considerably smaller scale.

Denmark's African partners receiving assistance are Botswana, the Congo, Ethiopia, Ghana, Kenya, Lesotho, Malawi, Morocco, Mauritius, Nigeria,

Swaziland, Tanzania, Tunisia, Uganda, the United Arab Republic, and Zambia. At present there are 59 Danish development projects and activities in Africa. Among the new ones are a project for adult education in Uganda ($840,000), a project for the promotion of pork production ($386,666), a domestic-science institute ($404,000), and a Faculty of Architecture building (£600,000) in Kenya, a technical-education centre ($333,333) and an audio-visual institute ($393,333) in Tanzania, and a food-control project in Zambia ($373,333).

The development assistance provided by *Norway* is concentrated on Kenya, Tanzania, Uganda, and Zambia. Almost 40 per cent of the total bilateral aid provided by Norway goes to Africa. The Norwegian bilateral aid to these countries is mainly concerned with educational programmes and is characerized by a close relationship between technical assistance and capital aid. In connection with the personnel provided under the technical-assistance agreements with the East African countries, the East African Community and the universities of East Africa, comparatively large amounts have been granted for the construction of buildings, the installation of heavy equipment and other capital inputs. Norway also participates in a fisheries training project in Ghana and is planning an agricultural project in the Malagasy Republic. Since 1964, Norway has financed consultancy services to an industrial probject in Tunisia and in 1970 $280,000 were granted to this country for a housing programme. Contributions have also recently been made to non-profit-making Norwegian organizations for health projects in Tanzania, Uganda, Ethiopia and the Congo (Kinshasa), for educational projects in the Congo (Kinshasa), the Malagasy Republic, Ethiopia and Lesotho, and for agricultural projects in Algeria, Nigeria and the Cameroons.

Finland's activities have mostly been linked with the joint Scandinavian projects in Africa, one of which Finland administers in Tanzania. A major part of its effort is, however, now directed to Tanzania in the form of experts, operational personnel, and volunteers. In Tunisia Finland has trained for several years forestry technicians, foremen and workers in the government service. A school for them has been built with Finnish assistance at Remel, near the Tunisian capital, in addition to which Finland has provided Tunisia with heavy and light forest equipment to be used in forestry training. There has also been a significant increase of Finland's technical personnel in Africa, which totalled 84 people in September 1970. There are 22 Finnish experts participating in the joint Scandinavian projects in Kenya and Tanzania (in 1970) and 16 Finnish experts are working under the bilateral arrangements in Ethiopia, Tanzania and Tunisia, as are 36 volunteers in Tanzania.

Joint Nordic projects

The co-operation between the Scandinavian countries in development assistance dates from 1955. The first venture of this kind was an agreement on the construction of a National Medical Centre in Korea and was signed in 1956 by the Government of South Korea, the United Nations Korean Reconstruction Agency, and the Governments of Denmark, Norway and Sweden. The functions of the Scandinavian Board for this project were defined in an agreement between the three Scandinavian governments. In Africa the first experiment in Scandinavian co-operation was the very successful Scandinavian Joint Expedition to Sudanese Nubia in 1960-4, which worked in the UNESCO Campaign to Save the Monuments of Nubia.

Co-operation in development-assistance matters between the Scandinavian countries is extensive, beginning with the Nordic Council[14] and a special ministerial committee for these matters, set up in 1961, and extending to regular periodical meetings between the officials working in the Scandinavian development-assistance offices. For instance, the directors of these authorities meet about four times each year to co-ordinate their respective programmes and to discuss the administrative details of the common development projects. Similarly, officials working at different levels in the Scandinavian aid offices exchange information and co-ordinate procedures in their own meetings.

The year 1970 saw the handling over of the Nordic Tanganyika Project to the Tanzanian authorities, who are now continuing it under the name of the Kibaha Education Centre. It consists of a secondary school for 550 pupils, an agricultural training centre (which had more than 700 pupils during 1970) and a health centre (which cared for some 200,000 patients).

The Nordic Co-operative Project in Kenya, sponsored jointly by Denmark, Finland, Norway and Sweden — a five-year $10-million undertaking now in its third year — is mainly concerned with co-operative education and training, and the running of a co-operative college. The project is administered by Kenya, and Denmark administers the Scandinavian contribution. Another project of a similar type was embarked upon in 1968 by Sweden and Denmark in Tanzania. Finland is to join in 1971.

The most recent Nordic project is an agricultural project based in Mbeya, Tanzania. The first phase of the project, consisting of a socio-economic survey of the Mbeya region, was finished during 1970. The project is planned to consist of a research station, a Ministry of Agriculture training station and a rural training centre and is estimated to cost $12 million in the period 1970-7, of which the Nordic countries will contribute two-thirds. The project is administered by Finland.

II. THE MACHINERY FOR THE ADMINISTRATION OF DEVELOP-MENT AID

Sweden

The overall organization for the planning and implementing of multilateral aid is the responsibility of the Ministry of Foreign Affairs. The planning and the implementation of the bilateral assistance programme is entrusted to a government agency, the Swedish International Development Authority (SIDA), which came into existence in 1965. The SIDA is the central authority for the administration of the Swedish bilateral-aid programme, whether it is concerned with technical or financial assistance or is of a humanitarian character. It is an independent agency, governed by a board of eight members presided over by the Director-General, who is appointed by the Government for a period of 6 years, which may be extended. The Director-General is a Civil Service appointee. The fact that the Social Democratic Party in Sweden has been in power for almost 40 years has considerably diminished the differences between political and Civil Service appointments which exist in countries with frequent changes of governments, usually followed by changed in the key posts of the administration. The members of the board of the SIDA are all appointed by the Government and are chosen from among the representatives of the major political parties, trade unions, industry, commerce and finance and the co-operative movement.

SIDA's policy is determined by the Swedish Parliament, to which the SIDA through the Government submits its annual requests for funds. In the field of international relations the SIDA falls within the competence of the Ministry of Foreign Affairs, under the auspices of which it conducts its dealings with recipient countries or international organizations and institutions. In constitutional terms the SIDA is directly responsible to the Government, in which the treaty-making power is vested. The staff of the SIDA has grown from 30 employees in 1962 to over 300 in 1970.[15] During the last two years the SIDA has established local offices (DAO) in the recipient countries receiving substantial amounts of Swedish development aid, such as Ethiopia, Tanzania, Kenya, Zambia and Tunisia. In 1970 a special Office for International Assistance was set up within the Ministry of Foreign Affairs and was headed by an Under-Secretary of State.

Denmark

Until 1971, Danish development assistance was administered by the Board for Technical Assistance, operating under the Ministry of Foreign Affairs. The Board consisted of representatives of various interested ministries, such as Finance, Trade, Agriculture, Education, etc. The overall supervision was vested in a Council for Development Assistance, composed of persons nominated by various institutions, both public and private, and appointed by the Minister of Foreign Affairs.

The Minister of Foreign Affairs was responsible for all aid matters and submitted proposals concerning the granting of development assistance to the Financial Committee of the Danish Parliament for approval. With the growth of the development-assistance administration, many of the responsibilities of the Foreign Minister were gradually delegated to the Board and left to be executed by its secretariat, which later became a special body called the Danish International Development Authority (DANIDA). An interesting feature of the Danish organization for development assistance was the creation of a special separate body called "International Co-operation" and charged with the task of disseminating information within Denmark about the scope and content of Danish development aid and about the recipient countries.

A commission of government officials and social scientists was set up by the Government in April 1970 to review Danish development-assistance policies for the purpose of revising the Danish aid legislation (the Act on Technical Co-operation with Developing Countries of 1962, as subsequently amended). The commission's recommendations were considered in the Danish Parliament in December 1970, together with a bill providing for the establishment of a new organization for development aid called the "Organization for International Development Co-operation". A statute establishing a ministry was tabled in Parliament on December 2, 1970. The terms of reference of the new organization (Section 3 of the Bill) are to co-ordinate Danish governmental assistance activities, whether implemented in direct collaboration with developing countries or through international organizations. The Minister for International Development Co-operation (referred to in the Bill as "the Minister") has power to provide financial and technical assistance and will also direct the activities of the Institute for Development Research.[16] The Minister is to be assisted by two bodies: (*a*) a Board of International Development Co-operation (composed of nine members appointed by the Minister), which will have advisory functions, and (*b*) a Council of International Development Co-operation (composed of up to 75 members nominated by authorities, institutions and organizations which take a special interest in matters relating to assistance to developing countries). The function of the Council will be to supervise the Board's activities, to receive reports from the Board and to give advice and submit recommendations to the Minister.

An interesting innovation in the new Danish organization for development assistance is the establishment in 1967 of the Industrialization Fund for Developing Countries (Section 10 of the Bill). Funds derived from the net revenue of the customs duty levied on green coffee, coffee substitute with a content of coffee, and extract and essence of coffee are to be transferred to this Fund in order "to promote investments in developing countries in collaboration with Danish trade and industries". As from January 1, 1971, such transfers will represent 40 per cent of the above-mentioned net revenue from the customs duty, and from January 1, 1972, and in subsequent years the transfers will represent 50 per cent of the said revenue from the customs duty. The Fund may also receive contributions from trade organizations, individual enterprises or private persons in the form of cash or guarantee capital.

Finland

The planning and implementation of all official development assistance, whether multilateral or bilateral, is the responsibility of the Ministry for Foreign Affairs. In March 1965, a Bureau of Technical Assistance was established within the Political Department of the Foreign Ministry. Since then, practically all administrative tasks related to development assistance have been concentrated in the Bureau, which is bound to implement the policy decisions made by the President, the Government and the Parliament.

26

In 1968, the Government of Finland appointed a public commission (composed of 25 members with a special interest in matters related to assistance to developing countries) to prepare a draft plan for future Finnish assistance. The commission submitted its report to the Government in two parts, in 1968 and 1970. The findings of the commission have largely been taken into account in the Foreign Ministry's own long-term plan for development assistance, which outlines the eventual growth of official assistance toward the 1% target.

A new commission for development assistance was appointed in 1970 for a two-year term. Its mandate is to act as an advisory body to the Foreign Ministry in the planning and implementation of Finnish aid programmes. The commission has, at its first task, taken a stand in the organization of the administration of the Finnish aid programmes. It recommends a considerable strengthening of the present system, leading to the establishment of a special department for development co-operation within the Foreign Ministry. The commission recommends that the re-organization should take place as early as the beginning of 1972. However, it did not exclude the possibility of further re-organization in the coming years, taking the form of the establishment of a separate, independent, government agency for development assistance. At present, however, a close inter-relationship with the overall implementation of the Finnish foreign policy within the Foreign Ministry is considered more practicable by the commission.[17]

Norway

The body responsible for the administration and implementation of development aid is the Norwegian Agency for International Development (NORAD), which was established in April 1962, and placed administratively under the Ministry of Foreign Affairs. The present structure and status of the NORAD, confirmed by a Parliamentary decision of October 25, 1969, has been in existence from December 1, 1968. The NORAD is governed by an eight-member board of governors presided over by a chairman. The Board is appointed by the Government and includes the Director-General of the NORAD, who is the executive head of the Agency.[18]

The NORAD, which has the legal status of a directorate, is responsible for the drawing up of plans for the use and co-ordination of the whole of

Norway's official assistance to the developing countries and presents proposals for annual appropriations for development assistance, administers projects and recruits Norwegian personnel for work in developing countries. The NORAD also recruits volunteers for the Norwegian Volunteers Service and grants scholarships to individuals from the developing countries. It also supports projects sponsored by Norwegian non-profit-making organizations in developing countries and promotes co-operation between the developing countries and Norwegian industry.

Apart from its annual budget, the NORAD puts forward questions of a fundamental nature and questions concerning negotiations on agreements with other states to the Ministry of Foreign Affairs.

Proposals on bilateral financial assistance and on support on participation in international programmes and assistance organizations are also presented to the Ministry of Foreign Affairs.

The NORAD is assisted in its task by an advisory body called "Rådet for Direktoratet for utviklingshjelp" (Council of the Directorate for Development Aid), the statute of which was approved by Parliament on November 27, 1968. The Council, which has 20 members elected by Parliament, follows the work done by the Directorate, with the object of promoting understanding of and support for Norwegian collaboration with the developing countries. Under this heading the Council discusses the general guidelines for the Directorate's work and its more important plans. The Council acts as an advisory body to the Directorate, as regards information work and contact with the public and the large organizations on questions which are of importance for the Directorate's work. On its own initiative the Council gives advice and puts forward proposals on questions concerning the Directorate's work. It also deals with matters which are submitted to it by the Board of the Directorate or by its own members. The Council considers the annual report and accounts of the Directorate and passes its comments on the Ministry of Foreign Affairs. Since 1968 the NORAD has established local offices in Kenya, Tanzania, Uganda and Zambia.

III. TYPES OF DEVELOPMENT AGREEMENTS

The term "development agreement" in Scandinavian usage may be defined as the legal instruments by which the Scandinavian countries provide the means (loans, credits, undertaking of projects, supply of equipment, skills and experts), in order to help the recipient country to carry out or to sustain its own development efforts on terms which are more favourable than those of normal commercial or banking sources. There may be several types of documents (treaties, agreements, agreed minutes, exchange of letters), but they are the most important instruments which govern the implementation of projects and the co-operation between the partners in this process.

Generally, development co-operation agreements are negotiated in the same way as any other treaty. The exact procedure, however, varies with the subject matter of each instrument, whether it concerns a framework agreement or a special project, loan or credit. The question determining the holding of the preliminary negotiations is based on tentative discussions between representatives of the developing country concerned, usually in the capital of that country. In the case of Sweden, a definite invitation, even to preliminary negotiations, cannot be issued unless the Swedish Government has approved Swedish support for the project. Prior to the meeting, the draft documents concerning the proposals to be discussed are exchanged between the two parties.

At the first meeting the various parts of the proposals are discussed to the extent necessary to clarify the positions of the delegations. The actual detailed discussion is referred to a working committee. Then the draft is referred back to the plenary meeting of the two delegations, in which the remaining questions, if any, are solved. The heads of the delegations initial the final draft by which the negotiations are concluded. The drafts are then submitted for signature by the plenipotentiaries of each party, which may be preceded by a final meeting of the delegations. Matters which have been dealt with during the negotiations but are not included in the text of the agreement sometimes form the subject of Agreed Minutes of Proceedings or a Memorandum or are confirmed in an exchange of letters between heads of delegations.

The aims of these documents are (i) to define in exact legal form the goals and the extent of a project and the ways of its implementation, (ii) to define the obligations of the donor country, the receiving country and any other participant in the project, and (iii) to define the procedure for the co-operation between the parties.

There is no standard form for a development agreement, basically because there are many types of projects and activities. However, the following are the main types of agreements:

(1) *Agreements of a general character*, or "frame-work agreements", which provide a legal framework for the channelling of aid to be specified in subsequent arrangements between the contracting parties.[19] They are usually called "Agreements on Technical Co-operation". They do not deal with special projects but rather specify general conditions for the provision of personnel and material resources and − when concluded with international organizations − the amount of the financial resources.

On the national level in the donor countries these types of agreement also mean that decisions about projects and special agreements under the general terms specified in the documents can also be made by the agency or directorate and such decisions do not have to be taken at Cabinet or King-in-Council level.

Another example of an agreement of a general type on the technical-assistance side is trust-fund arrangements concluded with one of the United Nations specialized agencies for associate expert schemes or for the support of individual projects.[20]

(2) *Agreements concerning a specific programme or project* to be undertaken and completed in co-operation between the contracting parties. These agreements define the activities and the goal, both often being assembled in one administrative unit or concentrated geographically in one spot.[21]

This type includes (i) bilateral agreements concerning the granting of aid (usually a main agreement and a Plan of Operation and Annual Work Programmes and budgets), in which the contract period is from three to five years, and (ii) bilateral agreements concerning credits and loans (usually consisting of a Credit Agreement and a Description of the project, Standard Annexes with rules for the transfer of capital, credit capital, procurement rules and other special rules). Sometimes such agreements also contain clauses concerning the provision of personnel.[22]

(3) *Joint agreements between several donors and one recipient.* These may take the form of bilateral agreements, by which development aid is made available to recipient countries jointly with aid given or administrered by international organizations or one or more of the other Scandinavian countries. This organization or country also makes a bilateral agreement with the recipient country.[23] This type of agreement thus constitutes a complex of bilateral agreements interlinked by mutual references contained in the provisions of each agreement.

Joint financing operations with the World Bank, (IRBD), and its affiliate, the International Development Association, (IDA), have been a standard part of Scandinavian financial assistance programmes. The joint financing agreements normally provide for the following matters:

(i) A description of the project to be financed;

(ii) The allocation of the amount of the financing between Sweden and the Bank;

(iii) The allocation of the total financing to various categories of expenditure for the project;

(iv) The use of the proceeds of the joint financing and the methods and procedures for procurement of goods and services financed thereunder;

(v) A procedure for submission to, and review by, the Bank of applications for disbursement of the joint financing and co-ordination of such disbursements;

(vi) The obligations of the recipients of the joint financing, with respect to the execution, operation and aministration of the project, and the supervision of the project by Sweden and the Bank;

(vii) An authority for the Bank to act on behalf of Sweden.

At present, every third development credit is offered jointly with the World Bank or the IDA. Since 1968 similar developments have taken place, for example, in the Swedish technical-assistance programme. Arrangements have been made for channelling Swedish assistance funds through several international organizations, thereby adding a multilateral tone to the Swedish bilateral technical-assistance programme. There is, however, very little room for bargaining in treaty negotiations with any organization of the United Nations family. The agreements to which these organizations are parties have been so standardized that the recipient states hardly have any choice but to accept their form and terms.

For example, the group of agreements concluded with the International Bank for Reconstruction and Development tend to be rigid, although the standard terms of these agreements have been carefully worked out by the Bank in co-operation with its member states. The question arises just how much the Plan of Operation which sets out the particulars of each project and which is incorporated into the Special Fund Agreement can actually alter the basic standard terms.

Joint agreements between several Scandinavian countries and the recipient African country co-ordinate the development aid of the countries concerned in connection with a specific project.[24] Under these agreements a joint consultative committee is set up, consisting of representatives appointed by each contracting party to serve as an advisory body and submitting regular reports on these projects.

IV. THE GENERAL TERMS AND CONDITIONS UNDER WHICH SCANDINAVIAN FINANCIAL AID IS PROVIDED

The policy of the Scandinavian countries with respect to the terms and conditions under which they provide their aid and assistance stems from their uniform support for the resolution adopted at the Second United Nations Conference on Trade and Development (UNCTAD II) on March 28, 1968.[25] Sweden, Denmark, Norway and Finland were among the developed countries which considered that *either* (*a*) the developed countries might provide 80 per cent more of their official aid in the form of grants *or* (*b*) they might provide 90 per cent of their official aid commitments as grants or loans at 2.5 per cent or less, with a repayment period of 30 years or more and a minimum period of grace of eight years.

The standard terms for *Swedish* development credits were formerly 2 per cent with a repayment period of 25 years and a period of grace of 10 years. Since the fiscal year 1967-8 Sweden has complied with the terms set forth by the International Agency for Development, by extending the credits for the period of 50 years at $\frac{3}{4}$ per cent interest.[26] Loans are made and are repayable in Swedish crowns.

In the case of *Denmark* all loans made in 1969 were interest-free, with an amortization of 25 years, including a seven-year period of grace. These terms have been generally applied since 1967.

Norway, in one of its latest agreements (concluded with Kenya in 1969), provided a credit of $1,390,000 at $\frac{3}{4}$ per cent interest with a repayment period of 50 years and a period of grace of 10 years.

In the case of *Finland* it has been suggested that the terms should normally be in keeping with the relevant OECD and UN recommendations, with an interest rate around 2 or 3 per cent, maturity after 25-30 years and an initial period of grace from 5 to 7 years.[27]

The problem of the tying of aid

An important aspect of any development aid and assistance, especially in connection with soft loans and credit terms, is the question of ties of either a political or an economic character. While the question of any direct political ties attached to the Scandinavian assistance to Africa does not really arise, the economic ties which do occur reflect the various attitudes of the Scandinavian countries towards the issue of membership of the EEC. There are various ways in which loans and credits may be tied to certain conditions or stipulations under which the credit is given. The most common are procurement conditions, that is, the loan or the part of it that is earmarked for the procurement of capital or other goods must be used in a special country. One can probably differentiate between five types of procurement tying of an official credit, as follows:

	Types of goods	Firm	Country
(1)	Specified in detail	Specified	Specified
(2)	Specified in detail	Free	Specified
(3)	Specified in detail	Free	Specified
(4)	Free	Free	Specified
(5)	Free	Free	Free

In loans of type (1), goods specified in detail must be procured from a specified firm in a specified country. Loans of type (2) are somewhat freer, as the buyer may choose the firm, which, of course, is only of interest if there are several competing firms of equal size or capacity in the branch that interests the buyer. Loans of type (3) may be used for the procurement of broadly defined categories of goods (for example, "machines and other capital goods") from any firm in the donor country. In type (4) there is only the provision that the loan must be used for procurement in the donor country and in type (5) this limitation is also abolished.

An interesting point worth mentioning in connection with the tying of credits to procurement is that most credit agreements have a clause which states that the principal of the loan and the interest on the credit shall be paid without deduction of any taxes, charges or fees which may be imposed under the laws of the country receiving the credit.

In no case, in which there is a procurement clause in connection with the credit, is there any corresponding clause concerning the duties, export, fees or other levies that the laws of the donor country may impose on the goods bought with the credit.

The absence of any clause protecting the recipient country from a change in the taxation and price policies of the donor country leaves the door open to the possibility that the purchasing value of the credit may thus be substantially reduced.[28]

The UNCTAD II Conference recognized that tying restricts the developing countries' opportunities of benefiting from the price and quality advantages which normally accrue from a free choice of suppliers. This is particularly the case when restrictions are imposed not only as regards the source of the goods but also as regards their nature. Furthermore, tying tends to reduce the real value of aid, in as much as the definition and the choice of the projects and the technology best suited to the requirements of the developing countries are limited.[29]

While there is no kind of political tie in any agreement concluded by any Scandinavian country in Africa, the approach, as far as tying aid to certain conditions of an economic character is converned, is not uniform.

The *Swedish* credits earmarked for projects are tied to the actual implementation of the project, but the Swedish development credits are not tied to procurement, and attempts have even been made to ensure that the procurement is open to international competition.

The practice in this direction was formerly not free from the objection that it gave Sweden certain priorities.[30] However, it has since been considerably improved, as is amply shown in one of the most recent credit agreements with Tanzania – that concerning a grain-storage project.[31] While the recent grants and credits are already free of any ties, in the case of technical assistance the very nature of the assistance provided presupposes the supply and use of both the expert personnel and the equipment from the donor country. Thus grants related to commodity assistance have consisted of Swedish goods (foodstuffs, paper, fertilizer) (Westring, op.cit., p. 279).

Norway too has pursued a policy of non-tied aid, although, as was pointed out in the 1969 *Survey of Norway's Aid to the Developing Countries*, "demands for tying loans to protect traditional Norwegian exports against discrimination due to tied aid deliveries have increased, however, as instances of such discrimination have been clearly demonstrated".[32]

Finland is rather a special case, as no credits were given up to 1970. In the future, procurement will necessarily be tied to Finnish sources, but it is envisaged that the bulk of the purchases will be expected to be made in Finland.[33]

Danish government loans to developing countries have to a great extent been of type (3) in the above-mentioned table.[34] Several agreements have allowed 25% of the total loan to be used elsewhere than in Denmark. It should also be mentioned that tying has not been restricted to Danish firms, and foreign companies registered in Denmark of their branches in Denmark may also compete. There has also always been complete freedom of choice of transport and shipping companies for the exporter and in this respect the national interest has been given lower priority than freedom of shipping.

A mild form of tying of aid has been considered in Denmark to establish a balance between the interests of the donor and those of the recipient country: the recipient country is entitled to choose the projects for which it will use the loans, and is also free to choose most of the capital goods it wants to buy. This procedure at the same time meets the export interests of the donor.

This practice is supposed to create a healthier climate between the parties and to even out the difference between the idealistic motives, on the one hand, and the gratitude, on the other. It is believed that, by admitting the economic interests of the donor, an atmosphere of openness is created, which in turn prevents the misuse of funds.

However, the risks involved in tying aid are obvious. The involvement of international capital and trade interests in Africa and the amounts of profit that are taken out of Africa in combinations of trade and aid are well known; the balance is always to the benefit of the donor.

It should be borne in mind that, if trade interests were allowed to suggest and choose projects, the risk would be that a number of small projects would be chosen only on the ground of their profitability to the export industry.

The argument in Denmark has been that, as long as these types of projects are under the control of the government and the assistance-giving agency, there is no danger in tying loans and credits, which, after all, are few and on a small scale. Provided however, that the new aid legislation is passed, Denmark will be in a position to extend development loans on more flexible conditions, as far as procurement is concerned.

V. THE NATURE OF THE OBLIGATIONS OF THE CONTRACTING PARTIES TO THE DEVELOPMENT AGREEMENT

It stems from the character of the development agreements that the burden of the obligation with respect to their implementation largely rests with the recipient country. This is true in particular in the case of credit agreements, in which the responsibility of the lender is met by simply making the credit available, while compliance with the conditions under which the credit can be used largely constitutes the obligation of the borrower. The fact that one party to the agreement is a donor (or a supplier of assistance under favourable conditions) has an impact on the sovereign equality of the recipient *vis-a-vis* the supplier, who is in a position to determine the conditions under which aid is granted to a much greater extent than the country which is receiving it. In this connection it is necessary to point out that all agreements concluded by the Scandinavian countries on technical assistance are called agreements *on co-operation*. From the legal point of view this is done to emphasize that, although in practice the agreement is to benefit only one party, the sovereign equality of both parties is fully respected.

The essence of the co-operation under these types of agreement has often been formulated in an article entitled "undertakings by the two Governments". The party providing the assistance undertakes to make available to the government of the recipient country such staff, material and resources as shall in each case be determined by the two contracting parties or the competent authorities appointed by each contracting party respectively. The recipient government undertakes to ensure effective utilization of the assistance provided, that is, the staff, resources and opportunities. In a way, this is a logical and rather superfluous provision, as the determination of the best use of the assistance has often been essential for carrying out national economic-development plans and projects, which were the primary motive for seeking the aid in the first place. The interest of the party providing the assistance in seeing that it is most efficiently used is twofold. Firstly, the country making the contribution will naturally wish to see that its assistance really serves its purpose and thus satisfies the motives for which the aid or assistance was granted. Secondly, there is the responsibility of the authority in charge of the implementation of the aid and assistance programme to the taxpayers in its own country. Thus, Swedish authorities dealing with development assistance matters are required by law to examine how aid appropriations have been spent and make necessary adjustments in their future plans in the light of international debate. They are, of course, also required to inform both the elected representatives and the public on these matters.

In the Swedish view the question of effectiveness is "the main criterion for selecting instruments and forms of aid".[35] Similarly, the Swedish Minister of Foreign Affairs stressed efficiency as a primary condition for Swedish assistance in an address to Parliament in 1967. He said that assistance entails the study of the receiver's situation, the mobilization of the donor's personnel and material resources, negotiation and agreement with the receiver, steering, checking and, last but not least, evaluation of results. "Sweden would have to partake in all these activities, if we wanted some assurance that the Swedish contributions were useful."[36]

It is the co-operation of both parties in making the best use of the assistance provided which is a criterion of their sovereign equality in terms of their responsibilities for the implementation of the development agreement in question. For example, a failure of the recipient government to make contributions to the project, such as local arrangements of all kinds (appropriation of land for construction, providing accommodation for the experts, transport and similar prerequisities) or to pay its share of the expenses incurred into the account set up for the project entitles the party providing the assistance to suspend its own activities or withhold further payment until the recipient party meets the obligations undertaken in the agreement.[37]

Needless to say, *bona fides* is an essential prerequisite for implementing any agreement in general and a development agreement in particular. Even when "supporting activities", such as legislative measures, road construction, land registration, power or water supply, etc. are specified in the "Plan of Operation" attached to the agreement, the *bona fides* element is indispensable.[38] It constitutes an important obligation on the part of the recipient country. To prevent any major differences arising in the course of the implementation of the development project, a suitable form of consultation and control, and of periodical reviews and progress reports is usually envisaged in the agreements, as well as provisions for the transfer of ownership of goods and buildings.[39]

The rights of the recipient party are asserted by its overall control, including the confirmation of appointments, of the personnel (experts, technicians, administrators), who are nationals of the party providing assistance. The recipient party invariably has the right to request the recall of any expert whose work or conduct is not satisfactory.[40]

Only in the agreement between Denmark and Tanzania of 1967 is there a provision concerning the conflict of interest that arises when an expert has access to findings or material which would be of use in the planning of the donor country. Such communication is allowed, provided the findings have been reported to the Government of Tanzania, do not prejudice the security of Tanzania or have not been classified as secret or confidential.

Whereas the technical expert provided under the development agreement is deemed to be equal in status to a member of the civil service in the recipient country, he is presumably also bound by the Official Secrets Act or its equivalent which applies to all state employees.

VI. STATUS OF THE PERSONNEL PROVIDED UNDER DEVELOPMENT AGREEMENTS

The question of the status of the personnel provided under the agreements is treated in great detail in all the development agreements concluded by the Scandinavian countries[41]. One of the most important aspects, however, of the implementation of a development agreement is the extent to which the foreign personnel should be employed and the supplier's training obligations. The need for the foreign personnel is determined by the need for technological and engineering know-how and the requirement of managerial skills. The donor country's concern for the success of the development project imples him to the rigorous employment of efficiency criteria. But considerations of efficiency are influenced by the policy of the government of the recipient country interested in the Africanization of the administration, including development projects. This is, of course, only possible provided the donor country conducts appropriate training programmes and counterpart programmes to form part of the technical assistance provided. The difficulties in finding counterparts and trainees are sometime considerable.

The status of the personnel (hereinafter referred to as "experts" for the sake of brevity) working in a recipient African country under a development agreement can be summed up as follows:

(1) The experts are the employees of the country providing the assistance, in accordance with their contract, which is governed by the law of their country.

(2) Their work in the country receiving assistance is a specific assignment, the conditions of which are determined on their behalf by their employer (the SIDA, DANIDA, NORAD or in the case of Finland, the Ministry of Foreign Affairs) in agreement with the recipient country.

(3) In the performance of their duties, they are, as a rule, under the direct authority of the government or agency in the recipient country.

The experts serve in the recipient country in various capacities as advisers, consultants or executive officers, the latter being called "operational personnel". Their position is the same as if they were in the direct employ of the respective body to which they are attached in the recipient country.[42]

It follows from all the agreements that the duties of experts assigned to work with the local authority (ministry, government, department or any other government body) do not differ from those of local executive officers of comparable rank.[43] However, the experts, whether they have advisory or operational functions, differ from their local counterparts in two important aspects:

(1) They enjoy exemption from the payment of taxes and related charges, and from the payment of customs duties. They also enjoy other privileges with regard to the exchange-control regulations, etc.

(2) They enjoy immunity from legal proceedings in respect of words spoken or written by them in their official capacities, unless it is a case of "gross negligence or wilful intention", and also in respect of civil liability, specified in "economic liability clauses", which constitute a standard provision in most of the development agreements entered into by the Scandinavian countries[44]. In this respect the development agreements concluded by the Scandinavian countries do not differ from each other.[45]

Tax and customs exemption and other economic privileges

The privileges concerning exemption from taxes, import duties and customs charges have differed from case to case and have sometimes been modified.[46] The provisions covering these privileges are very clear and each agreement develops them in great detail. Both tax- and customs-exemption clauses in the bilateral agreements have mainly the same functions, namely, to prevent an indirect transfer of funds from the sending country's government to that of the receiving country. Scandinavian personnel employed by the DANIDA, the NORAD, the SIDA and the Finnish Bureau are considered to be employees of the respective organization, which means that they are taxed in their home countries, and their position is regulated by a convention for the avoidance of double taxation between the countries. Customs exemptions usually fall into the category of first-arrival exemptions, that is, exemption from customs duties on household goods and personal effects and usually one car per family within six months of first arrival in the country of service. Subsequent imports are subject to excise. Free housing and in certain cases free transport, at least on official duty, are usually provided by the receiving countries.

It is, of course, quite understandable that the experts sent to work in Africa in connection with the development-assistance programme should be fully entitled to compensations of all kinds (financial, leave entitlement, housing, transport, etc.) arising out of their transfer to a country with a climate and living conditions very different from their own countries. It would be naive to assume that these experts could be recruited in the absence of substantial material incentives. What is less understandable is why benefits of this nature which the personnel from Denmark, Finland, Norway and Sweden receive should constitute an obligation of the recipient country rather than of their direct employers.[47] The official argument is that the agreements are agreements about development *co-operation* between the countries and that they share the expenses of projects, the main part of which is financed by the donor country.

Immunity from legal proceedings etc.

Immunity from legal proceedings is stipulated in much less clear terms. Let us give some examples. The Agreement between Norway and Ghana[48] states that "for the purposes of the regulations of the Government of the Republic of Ghana, all technical-assistance personnel provided and paid by the Government of the Kingdom of Norway shall be deemed to be legally resident in Norway". The question arises, however, as to whether the "regulations" also means the laws of Ghana and whether "legally resident in Norway" constitutes an exemption from legal proceedings in Ghana or whether the Norwegian personnel can be regarded as being "temporarily resident in Ghana" and, as such, subject to the regulations relating to aliens in conformity with the Ghanaian laws.

Although the legal status of the *Norwegian* personnel is specified in greater detail in the Agreement with Tanzania,[49] where, as already pointed out above, the operational officer is "in all respects a member of the Civil Service of Tanzania and shall be bound by the rules and regulations thereof", this provision is contradicted by privileges granted under the Agreement, which are not enjoyed by members of the Tanzanian Civil Service.[50]

42

Finnish expert personnel are not liable in espect of any damage to a third party caused in connection with the performance of the duties assigned to them under the Agreement (the recipient government is liable in their place).[51] In other instances not regulated by the Agreement, they are to comply with the laws, regulations and orders of the recipient government.[51]

The status of the *Danish* expert personnel in respect of exemptions from local jurisdiction has not been treated uniformly in the various agreements concluded by Denmark with the African recipients. The Danish Government, however, finds it imperative that its co-operation agreement should include a clause on partial immunity for its personnel serving in a developing country.

The Agreement between Denmark and Tanzania, which goes into great detail as far as exemptions from taxes and customs duties are concerned, is silent on the question of jurisdiction. However, there is a "most-favoured-nation" clause, which is also to be found in several other Danish agreements, as well as in the Finnish agreement with Zambia of 1970. The articles stipulate (in different wordings) that experts shall be treated in manner not less favourable than that enjoyed by experts assigned by other countries. This has been the standard provision of most U.S. agreements concerning development-assistance personnel and the Scandinavian countries, notably Denmark, have readily adopted it.

In a provision in the recent Danish agreement with Botswana (of November 16, 1970) Botswana is asked to ensure that the Danish experts shall enjoy the "full protection of the law". Similar provisions exist in other Danish agreements (as well as in Finnish agreements with Tanzania and Zambia).

The provision is strongly reminiscent of what is known in international law as the "capitulation treaties", based on the assumption that the institutions of a considerable number of States were inferior to or different from those of most European and American states and of Japan.[52]

Such provisions today leave the door open to the interpretation that the legal protection available to the citizens of Botswana, Tanzania, Zambia, etc., is not good enough for the experts from Denmark or Finland. The official argument for the inclusion of such provisions is that Danish and Finnish citizens should be accorded the same treatment and enjoy privileges which are not less that those enjoyed by the citizens of Botswana etc., in this respect. As a DANIDA official pointed out to the authors, experts should be protected against less developed legal and judicial systems by provisions of this character. The recruitment of experts is considered to be difficult without such provisions. (Obviously not as regards Ethiopia, as agreements with Ethiopia do not have this provision.) It can be argued that the philosophy behind this thinking is influenced by the "capitulation treaty" ideas. The fact that these "less developed legal and judicial systems" happen to have been introduced by Britain and France except in the case of Ethiopia and are therefore based on common law and the *code civil* has somehow not been taken into consideration.

The status of the Scandinavian personnel compared with that of other countries

On the whole, the status of the Scandinavian technical personnel working in Africa under agreements on technical co-operation does not differ very much from that of the experts of other countries, as has been shown by A.M. Lövgren in her paper on *Privileges and Immunities in Bilateral Technical Co-operation.*[44] One may, however, ask whether this should not be changed in the future. It does not follow that the system under which the experts work in Africa (under the auspices of international organizations or bilateral arrangements) is an ideal one. In a way, the present-day experts have replaced the members of the Colonial Service, which constituted the core of the administration of each African country prior to independence. The privileges which the colonial officers enjoyed were one of the outward symbols of colonial domination. Paradoxically enough, their privileges never reached the level of those enjoyed by the UN technical personnel or even of those accorded to the experts working under development-assistance agreements. With the attainment of independence, they were replaced by African Civil Servants, though the pace and extent of the Africanization of the government administration and technical services differed considerably from country to country.

Many African countries still continue to employ expatriate officers in their administration, government agencies and corporations under the terms set forth by the British Civil Service Commission or a comparable body in charge of appointments. Although these terms of service are financially more favourable than those of an African Civil Servant of comparable rank, they do not match the favourable conditions of the UN technical personnel or even the experts supplied under the development agreements.

When the first development agreements were drafted in the Scandinavian countries, there were already a number of precedents. All of them were influenced by the privileges and immunities granted to the personnel of the international organizations and by diplomatic immunities and privileges in general.[53]

It is understandable that the authors of bilateral technical-co-operation agreements should have been tempted to copy the diplomatic privileges and immunities and the privileges and immunities granted to officials of international organizations, in particular as the United Nations itself is a party to so many technical-co-operation agreements. This trend has led to the practice that the technical experts (including those of the United Nations) are granted privileges originally meant for officials of the United Nations, whose functions are fundamentally different from those of the expert. As A.M. Lövgren points out, the Convention on the Privileges and Immunities of the United Nations was not written to provide for the needs of United Nations technical-assistance experts, and it is unlikely that the assistance programmes were even conceived of, when the Convention was written. It was written to provide for the needs of the United Nations and all its officials.

The international official is working for an organization whose purpose is universal, the bilateral technical-assistance experts are subordinate to the interests of two sovereign countries, who are co-operating. The functions they are to fulfil and their legal situations are entirely different. In fact, they are so completely different that the immunities and privileges granted them cannot have the same function.

Bilateral technical-assistance experts are not diplomatic agents and do not fulfil the functions of diplomatic agents; they are not officials of the United Nations working to fulfil the purpose of the United Nations; they are officials or employees of one sovereign country, carrying out work in another sovereign country in the interests of both countries.

In so far as the experts are officials or employees of one government and are mainly or wholly financed by that government, and the immediate effect or advantage of the work of the expert is directed to the interests of the receiving country, it is impossible to regard them in all respects as ordinary aliens resident in the receiving country, from the viewpoint of both governments. But to accord to the experts a special status does not necessarily mean that they should be put almost on a par with diplomatic agents or United Nations officers. Any immunity, privilege and facility accorded the bilateral experts must be based on a necessity in relation to their work or the technical-co-operation programme as a whole. An excess of privileges and immunities for individuals who are already privileged, economically, socially and educationally certainly does not fit the principle of international solidarity, of which the technical-co-operation is supposed to be an expression.[54]

VII. THE SETTLEMENT OF DISPUTES

The machinery for the settlement of disputes, which plays such an important role in the private-investment and commercial-credit types of agreement is considerably less significant in the development agreements, the purpose of which is to provide aid or technical assistance. In practice, it has been included in the development agreements concerning credit, but it rarely appears in the development agreements of a general character.

The absence of any provision for the settlement of disputes in the development agreements of a general character is a corollary to the purpose of the agreement, described, for example, in the agreement between Denmark and Kenya as a desire to strengthen the friendly relations between the two countries and their peoples, "recognizing their mutual interests in the economic and technical development of their countries".[55]

The occurrence of disputes under the development agreements is almost inconceivable, considering the motives behind the whole concept of development assistance. Besides, each agreement contains a number of safety clauses that are intended to preclude disputes arising between the contracting parties which cannot be settled by negotiation. Thus, for example, the agreements provide for the possibility of recalling any expert whose work or conduct may have led to complaints. This can be done at the request of the recipient country or on the initiative of the sending government.[56] Another safeguard against the occurrence of disputes of a serious character is the provision on termination invariably included in all agreements. Both contracting parties have the right to terminate the agreement by giving six months' or a year's notice to the other party, as the case may be. The only agreements with elaborate provisions on the settlement of disputes are those concerning credit. These provisions are of a standard character and are copied from the provisions employed by the International Bank for Reconstruction and Development. An example of the procedure on the settlement of disputes is contained in one of the latest agreements between Sweden and Tanzania.[57] The procedure is identical with that envisaged in the Development Credit Agreement between Sweden and Ethiopia of June

3, 1969. In conclusion, it should be pointed out that, since the development-assistance programme started in the Scandinavian countries, there has not been one recourse to arbitration and no disputes have ever arisen out of the various development agreements which have not been settled by negotiations between the local representatives of the development agency and the authority in the recipient country or through diplomatic channels.

VIII. CONCLUSIONS

In summing up this brief outline of Scandinavian development assistance, as reflected in the development agreements, several points should be made.

(1) The agreements are undergoing continuous amendment, which reflects the change in the scope and content of the assistance and the trend towards shifting the administration of the various projects from the headquarters of the development agencies to their offices in the field and ultimately to the receiving countries themselves.

(2) The re-organization of the Scandinavian development authorities is likely to continue. These organizations will adapt themselves to the changing situation in which they are and will be working. There is, of course, always the danger that efficiency will decrease, due to increased bureaucratization and long-drawn-out administrative procedures. It sometimes takes more than 12 months to recruit an expert and get him into the field (and it takes 36 months before a major development project can get started). This, of course, reflects not only administrative difficulties but also difficulties in finding the right person with first-class qualifications in these small countries. Furthermore, one has to remember that Scandinavian assistance personnel have to work in a foreign language, and there are obvious difficulties in finding people who fulfil the language requirement, especially in French and Spanish.

(3) Increased pressure from the receiving countries to shorten the length of the administrative procedure, and to avoid unnecessary delay in project preparation is already being felt and will undoubtedly increase. One of the answers may well be an increased number of long-range economic and technical-assistance agreements, as envisaged in the recent Norwegian four-year programme, in accordance with which money has been allocated for a longer period than was the case before, to the benefit of the planning.

(4) Development assistance is never really free from politics and no doubt its aspects will continue to be challenged at various levels in each country. No doubt we shall have increased and more heated discussion on which countries should be chosen as partners in co-operation. It should be

recalled that over the last few years there has been increased opposition to giving aid to some African countries whose regimes are being criticized as too conservative or reactionary. The implication is that Scandinavian countries, by giving aid to these countries, are helping to strengthen their positions. The trend in switching aid to the "progressive" African countries is already noticeable.

(5) Denmark, Norway and Sweden are negotiating applications for some kind of association with the EEC. This is a very controversial issue in the countries themselves and caused the fall of one Norwegian government in March 1971. In the case of Sweden there is the question of the compatibility of its neutrality with association with such a close community of NATO countries. Finland's positions here is even more delicate.

Furthermore, the EEC is also an organization which discriminates against countries which are not members. Each member has to pay its share of the cost of the various EEC development organizations. For Sweden, for example, this would amount to about $20 million a year. This represents, of course, a kind of multilateral assistance but not the form of multilateral assistance that the Scandinavian countries prefer, that is, assistance channeled through the UN and its specialized agencies. Association with the EEC would thus mean limitations on these countries' opportunities of choosing their development partners.

(6) A much more important problem, however, is that the further increase of development aid and assistance will most likely be influenced by the national economic situation — definitely more so in the future than in the past. One may point to the Swedish example, as Gunnar Myrdal has done in his latest book *The Challenge of World Poverty*.[58]

The reason why the Swedes give aid and assistance is not primarily a matter of expanding a Swedish export market or any other economic consideration; it is basically a matter of solidarity. At least we would like to think so, and recent developments point in the same direction.

Strains in the economic situation in the US have always had immediate effects on the amount of aid voted by the Congress (which incidentally is the general assembly that is most sensitive to slight changes in public opinion). In this respect the Scandinavian countries have so far resisted this kind of economic pressure. Even during the present strained economic situation in Scandinavia, the development efforts have *not* decreased. On the contrary, the Scandinavian countries are continuing to pursue the goal of 1 per cent of their GNPs.[59] The Swedish Minister of Finance has suggested postponing the date until after 1975, with reference to the balance-of-payments situation. As the SIDA, because of its planning capacity, will probably have difficulties in using these funds in a meaningful way in 1974, they will probably not threaten the balance of payments. An alternative that has been suggested is that more funds should be channelled into international organizations, (without, however, discussing any efficiency criteria). According to Gunnar Myrdal, such countries as Sweden (he also mentions Canada and the Netherlands and in a similar category Switzerland, Austria and the other Scandinavian countries), whose motivations for giving aid are not primarily based on national egoistic grounds but on moral grounds, are continuing to increase their aid rather than to decrease it. If, however, the economic situation deteriorates during the years to come, it will be interesting to see how much international solidarity can be stretched and how much domestic political pressures will be brought to bear on the Scandinavian Parliaments.

(7) In this situation the information circulated to the general public about the aims of development co-operation — and special kinds of such information — is of the utmost importance. The development authorities in Scandinavia have accordingly allotted substantial sums in their budgets to information work in the next few years. But the general public's knowledge of and interest in foreign aid and related questions is, unfortunately, still rather small. This is the more striking if one looks at the outflow of information in the various mass media. There is a good deal of information to receive, but very little of it is received.[60]

Finally, a point should be made about one of the paradoxes of Scandinavian aid, notably in the case of Sweden, which has pledged its support for the states threatened by the white-minority regimes in southern Africa, while simultaneously increasing the volume of its trade with South Africa. An explanation of this phenomenon may be found primarily in the political and economic systems of the Scandinavian countries. They are capitalist states in which there is a certain amount of state ownership and state interference in the economy but in which the governments do not control private industry. Private industry in both Scandinavia and other capitalist states in the western world does business with South Africa and profits from doing so. The volume of the Scandinavian trade with South Africa, which is, needless to say, strongly criticized by large sections of the political movements in

Sweden, is, of course, very small compared with those of the countries which are really important for South Africa's economy, such as the USA, Great Britain, France and West Germany.[61]

The official argument is that a unilateral Scandinavian boycott of trade with South Africa would not hurt South Africa at all but only the Scandinavian countries. Another argument is that under the circumstances, when some African countries are themselves split over the question of "beginning a new dialogue with South Africa", Sweden should not be more African than the Africans themselves. These arguments are, of course, highly questionable, but it would be going beyond the scope of this paper to develop them here. The solution would seem to lie not in unilateral action but in the concerted action of the Security Council, whose resolution imposing a trade embargo on South Africa would give the Scandinavian governments the right to ban trade with South Africa, as they did in the case of Southern Rhodesia.

NOTES

1 Lord McNair, "The General Principles of Law Recognized by Civilized Nations", *British Yearbook of International Law*, London, 1957, Vol. 33.

2 See, for example, Algeria's Investment Code, Ordinance Nos. 66-284 of September 15, 1966; also *Investment Laws and Regulations in Africa*, UN Publication, 1965; and T.O. Elias, "The Law of Foreign Investments in Africa", *The Nigeria Bar Journal*, (1966), Vol. VII, p. 13; and more generally, Schwarzenberger, *Foreign Investments and International Law* (1969), esp. Chapter 7.

3 In his article "The Roots of Underdevelopment" in *Race Today* (London, August 1970), Robin Jenkins argues that, when Britain gives aid to a poor nation, it in fact subsidizes the export of manufactured products from Britain. There are good economic reasons for arguing that, instead of devaluing the pound, Britain should have given massive grants of aid in sterling to the poor nations. This would have created huge orders for goods to be exported to the poor nations and would have made them even more dependent on Britain in the future.

4 We do not think that, for example, the agreements between the LAMCO and Liberia, though undoubtedly advancing the industrial growth of Liberia, should be called development agreements in the real sense of the word, because the issue of the development of Liberia was never the reason for concluding them but rather the profit the LAMCO would make out of them.

5 The term "Scandinavian" has been consistently used by the authors of this paper to designate Sweden, Denmark, Norway and Finland, while "Nordic" has been used only in referring to an official title, project or document.

6 Gaitskell, quoted by Dr. K. Busia in his speech at Singapore, reported by *The Star*, Accra, January 30, 1971. Cf. also what the Director of the SIDA, Mr. Ernst Michanek, has said in his recent book *The World Development Plan* (Uppsala, 1971, p. 12): "Swedish foreign aid policy should properly be discussed in an international perspective. The tasks Sweden undertakes in the form of direct co-operation with the countries and regions of the world should be seen in a larger context. They must be planned, executed and evaluated as integral parts of a global effort."

7 Kungl. Maj:ts proposition Nr 100 of February 23, 1962. The history of Swedish development aid is treated in great detail by Klas Markensten in his book *Svensk u-landshjälp idag* (Stockholm: Almqvist & Wiksell, 1967, 183 pp.).

8 Kungl. Maj:ts proposition 1968:100 of May 28, 1968.

9 *Norway's Aid to the Developing Countries, Survey 1969,* published by the Norwegian Agency for International Development, Oslo, 1970, p. 9.

10 The presence of Scandinavia in Africa in 1970 is considerably different from that of 320 years ago, when a dispute between the Swedes and the Danes concerning a trading station on the Gold Coast (Christianborg) was one of the causes of the one of the frequent wars between the two countries. When a peace treaty was finally negotiated in 1660, Sweden was offered Iceland in lieu of its possessions in West Africa – a rather illuminating example of the type of early Scandinavian "collaboration". Scandinavian contacts with Africa in the past include, of course, more enlightened ventures than disputes about slave-trade stations. The Swedish natural scientists of the 18th century, C.P. Thunberg and Adam Afzelius, were followed by the missionaries a hundred years later – the Swedes set out for Ethiopia and the lower reaches of the River Congo and the Finns for Amboland in South-West Africa. The Norwegians created the largest mission field of them all – the Norwegian Missionary Society's stations in Madagascar. Later came the Danish missions in Nigeria and the Congo. Some very important research results in African linguistics and investigations of prophetic movements have come out of these missions. Natural sciences and missionary work – these are the basic features in the long-standing Scandinavian interest in Africa. There were, of course, also the anthropologists, such as Gerard Lindblom and Edward Westermarck. There were also the merchants and industrialists concentrating on North and South Africa and on selling specialities such as matches, ball-bearings and electrical equipment.

11 In 1970 the Swedish Government and the Social Democratic Party contributed funds to the school of the Frente de Libertacão de Moçambique (FRELIMO) in Dar es Salaam, the Mozambique Institute, the Zimbabwe Welfare Trust, South West African Peoples' organization (SWAPO), and the Partido Africano da l'Independencia de Guine e Cabo Verde (PAIGC). The Swedish Government also established a special fund to assist refugees from southern Africa. Denmark uses similar funds to support refugee schools in Botswana and Swaziland. Norway gave $28,000 to the Mozambique Institute in 1969. In this connection it is worth while mentioning the recent unanimous recommendation of the Council of the Norwegian Agency for International Development (NORAD), made in April 1970, that this type of aid should be continued. Furthermore, the Council, by a majority vote, adopted the following resolution: "The Council is also of the opinion that these formal requirements [that, as a fundamental principle, the aid should go to a public authority in the recipient country] must not prevent Norway from giving support, as a link in its development policy, to projects set on foot by larger popular organizations and movements working for national and social liberation." Similar contributions have been made in Finland through the UN channels.

12 During 1968-9, Danish public contributions amounted to $2,520,000, of which $200,000 was spent on stock-fish deliveries, and private contributions amounted to $2,346,667. Up to May 1970, Finnish public contributions amounted to $261,967 and private contributions amounted to $490,248. Norwegian public contributions amounted to $11,188,811, of which stock-fish deliveries made up the largest part, and private contributions amounted to $4,475,524. In January 1970 an additional $839,161 for relief was granted by the Norwegian Parliament. Total Swedish public grants amounted to $3,972,868, of which $3,488,372 was contributed before the civil war ended (the contributions in 1968-9 amounted to $2,422,480). Private contributions amounted to about $8 million.

13 Most recently this discussion has been re-opened in Norway. See, for example, O. Stokke, "The Selection of Countries for Development Co-operation", in *Internasjonal politikk*, Oslo, 1970, No. 4 (December), pp. 375-397.

14 The Nordic Council is a permanent institution consisting of 69 members of the Nordic Parliaments and a varying number of ministers from each Nordic country. The Council was established in 1952 as a forum for consultations between the Parliaments and Governments of the Nordic countries on issues of mutal interest.

15 For the organization of the SIDA, see the chart in Annex VI.

16 The object of the Institute, as specified in Section 12 (1) of the Bill, is "to undertake, promote and publish studies of problems relating to the development of developing countries in economic, social and other community fields, to collect documentation, and to follow current research in Denmark and abroad in this field".

17 See also Jaakko Iloniemi's article "Finland and International Development Co-operation", *Finnish Trade Review*, Januari, 27, 1971.

18 For the organization of the NORAD, see the chart in Annex VII.

19 In the words of Article 1 of the Agreement on Technical Co-operation between the Government of the Kingdom of Denmark and the Government of the Republic of Botswana of November 16, 1970, "the Government of Denmark will make available to the Government of Botswana such personnel, material resources and training opportunities as shall in each case be determined by the two Parties".

20 For example, the Agreement between the Government of Sweden and the Food and Agriculture Organization of the United Nations of January 14, 1969. The purpose of this Agreement was to set up a procedure to enable the Organization to enter into commitments on the strength of Swedish contributions to projects chosen in consultation between the SIDA and the Organization. The Agreement furthermore specifies the manner in which the Swedish contributions will be made available and the way in which the Organization will handle the funds and account for them.

21 For example, the Agreement of June 26, 1964, between the Government of Denmark and the Government of Kenya on the establishment of a women's college in Nairobi.

22 In a Development Credit Agreement between the Government of Sweden and the Government of the United Republic of Tanzania, the lender (Sweden) is to make available to the borrower (Tanzania) a credit to the amount of 20 million Swedish crowns to assist in the financing of a project for the development of grain-storage facilities in Tanzania. The details of the projects are contained in the Annex, which constitutes an integral part of the Agreement.

23 Westring, G.: "Swedish Aid to Developing Countries", in *Journal of World Trade Law*, London 1970, Vol. 4, No. 2, p. 270. An example of such a complex of agreements is the following four instruments: the Guarantee Agreement (Fourth Telecommunications Project) between the Empire of Ethiopia and the International Bank for Reconstruction and Development of June 3, 1969; the Joint Financing Agreement between the Empire of Ethiopia, the Kingdom of Sweden, the International Bank for Reconstruction and Development and the Imperial Board of Telecommunications of Ethiopia of June 3, 1969; the Development Credit Agreement (Fourth Telecommunications Project) between the Kingdom of

Sweden and the Empire of Ethiopia of June 3, 1969; the Loan Agreement (Fourth Telecommunications Project) between the International Bank for Reconstruction and Development and the Imperial Board of Telecommunications of Ethiopia of June 3, 1969, and the General Administration Letter between Sweden and the Bank of the same date.

24 The Agreement between the Governments of Denmark and Sweden and the Government of Tanzania on Co-operative Assistance to Tanzania of July 18, 1968.

25 Resolution 29 (II) on Improving the Terms and Conditions of Aid for Alleviating the Problems of External Indebtedness. For the text of the Resolution, see the Proceedings of the United Nations Conference on Trade and Development, Second Session, New Delhi, 1 February to 29 March 1968, Volume I (Report and Annexes), p. 40 ff. See also the statement of the Danish Minister of Foreign Affairs, Mr. P. Hartling, at the 66th Plenary Meeting of the UNCTAD II on March 12, 1968 (Proceedings, p. 104), the statement of the Finnish Minister of Trade and Industry, Mr. O. Salonen, at the 44th plenary meeting on February 6, 1968 (Proceedings, p. 109), the statement of the Norwegian Minister of Commerce and Shipping, Mr. K. Willoch, at the 46th plenary meeting on February 7, 1968 (Proceedings, p. 153) and the statement by the Swedish Minister of Commerce, Mr. G. Lange, at the 44th plenary meeting on February 6, 1968 (Proceedings, pp. 170-172).

26 These conditions were applied, for example, to the above-mentioned Development Credit Agreement with Tanzania concerning the grain-storage project and in four joint financing operations with the IDA in Ethiopia, Tunisia, Kenya and Tanzania. The following are the joint operations with the IDA in Africa:
1. Development Credit Agreement (Second Tunisia Water-Supply Project) between the Kingdom of Sweden and the Republic of Tunisia, dated June 30, 1970.
2. Development Credit Agreement (Fourth Highway Project) between the Kingdom of Sweden and the Empire of Ethiopia, dated January 15, 1968.
3. Development Credit Agreement (Livestock Development Project) between the Kingdom of Sweden and the Republic of Kenya, dated Semptember 26, 1968.
4. Development Credit Agreement (Tan-Zam Highway Project) between the Kingdom of Sweden and the United Republic of Tanzania, dated February 24, 1969.

27 Se note 17.

28 M. Boserup, *Hjælper vi?*, Copenhagen 1967, p. 124; I. Foighel, *Utviklingsbistand*, Copenhagen 1970, p. 48.

29 UNCTAD II, Proceedings, p. 41.

30 The earlier agreements, for example, the agreements between Sweden and Tanzania of September 24, 1965, on credit for rural water supplies and buildings for co-operative education or the agreement between Sweden and the Sudan of January 6, 1966, on a credit for rural water supplies, provided that Swedish suppliers should be given adequate opportunities of tendering for the goods and services to be financed out of the proceeds of the credit, and no less favourable treatment than that accorded to suppliers from other countries. However, under these agreements the recipient country was obliged to pass the copies of the invitations to tender to the local Swedish Embassy and furthermore "the special adviser to the executing agency, who was also the SIDA's man on the spot", was given an oppor-

tunity to study all the relevant tenders and to present his comments and recommendations on all phases of the procurement (Westring, G., op.cit., p. 283). This type of control over the procurement procedure was subsequently abolished.

31 Procurement on the basis of international competition is governed by the following rules embodied in provisions 4.1-4.3 in the Exchange of Letters No. 2, which constitutes an integral part of the agreement:
   4.1. Invitations to tender, specifications, draft contracts and all other tender documents will be drafted so as not to exclude any potential bidder.
   4.2. Bidders will be given a minimum period of 60 days, from the issue of the invitation to tender, in which to submit their tenders.
   4.3. Invitations to pre-qualify and to tender shall include advertising in newspapers of general circulation in Tanzania, Kenya and Uganda, as well as written notices in four copies to all permanent diplomatic missions in Dar-es-Salaam.
   The only right reserved to the SIDA, which is, of course, in conformity with the SIDA's overall responsibility for the implementation of the agreement, is contained in section 4.4 of the aforesaid letter:
   4.4. Contracts will be awarded to the bidder who shall have submitted the lowest evaluated tender. If the SIDA shall so request, the Borrower shall transmit to the SIDA for comments a copy of the evaluation of bids and the proposal for award of contract before the final selection of supplier is made. The comments shall be made by the SIDA within fifteen days of receipt of such copy.

32 The Survey, published by the Norwegian Agency for International Development (Oslo, 1970), does not give any details of the cases of discrimination mentioned, neither does it suggest that Norwegian policy will change in the future.

33 Extract from Mr. Jaakko Iloniemi's article (note 17). Mr. Iloniemi is the Director of the Bureau of Technical Assistance of the Finnish Foreign Office. In another article, "Finland and International Economic Aid", published in the *Bank of Finland Monthly Bulletin*, (11, Helsinki, 1968, p. 4), he mentions another interesting factor influencing Finland's aid policy:
   "It is customary to presume that the economy of an aid donor is diversified and that the exports of the donor consist of highly processed industrial products. This is not entirely true in the case of Finland. The structure of her exports is still rather one-sided and she is a net importer of capital. The development of the balance of payments and the adaptation of the economy to international competition are factors which should be taken into consideration when the volume of resources, or the forms of aid to be extended are being planned."
   He also points out that in the case of Finland more aid from Finland would amount to a net outflow of convertible currencies from the country and thus become a real burden on the balance of payments. It would also burden the economy as a whole, because, under this assumption, it would not increase employment in the country.

34 According to the Danish memorandum containing the annual aid review for 1970, submitted to the Development Assistance Committee of the Organization for Economic Co-operation and Development on July 24, 1970 (DAC/AR(70) 1/50), the effects of tying are mitigated in the following ways:
   (1) The lists drawn up in the agreements are of an indicative nature; this implies that a borrowing country may obtain amendments to the list of changes, if the priorities of its development plan or other factors, such as price relations, make this desirable;

(2) There is no fixed rule as to the Danish content of the equipment concerned; the rule has been administered liberally, and purchases of equipment with considerable contents of foreign components have been financed in several cases;
(3) In some cases the procurement of spare parts has been financed under loan agreements;
(4) Transport costs are usually financed under loan agreements and are never procurement-tied;
(5) In some cases, though not in 1969, 25 per cent of the proceeds has been non-tied. This provision has been applied in relation to countries in the lowest income categories.

35 See the review of the Swedish aid programme for 1966 submitted to the Development Assistance Committee of the OECD (DAC/AR(66) 1/18).

36 Quoted by G. Westring, op.cit., p. 274.

37 The conditions under which the lender is entitled to suspend or ultimately cancel the credit are elaborated in the Agreement between Sweden and Tanzania of July 2, 1970, in the following way:
(a) A default shall have occurred in the payment of principal or interest under the Agreement or under any other financial commitment entered into by the borrower in relation to the lender.
(b) The borrower shall have failed to meet any other obligation under the Agreement and shall not have rectified such failure upon notice by the lender.
(c) An extraordinary situation shall have arisen which shall make it improbable that the borrower will be able to perform its obligations under the Agreement.

38 For example, Article VI (2) of the Agreement between Sweden and Ethiopia of Semptember 8, 1967, concerning co-operation in the project to establish suitable methods of regional agricultural development in Ethiopia and to train staff for this purpose, states that "the imperial Ethiopian Government shall endeavour to carry out such land reform and other measures as may induce improved agricultural productivity in the Project Area". Some of these measures, such as the construction of roads, the establishment of local health centres etc., are specified in the operational plan and some have to be left to the discretion of the recipient country, which is supposed to be sufficiently interested in the project to adopt them to the best of its ability.

39 The early Swedish technical-assistance agreements usually instituted a separate organization under the joint control of Sweden and the receiving state. The joint control body normally consisted of one special representative of each of the two co-operating parties, the Swedish representative being the local Swedish ambassador. It was soon found that these joint control bodies tended to become isolated from the receiver's administration, and problems arose in transforming them into a regular part of this administration. In fact, such a body might be regarded as an international organization, as long as it remained under the joint control of two states, a fact that naturally impeded its ultimate "nationalization". The system was furthermore often coupled with an over-optimistic belief in the capacity of the board of the joint control body to solve policy problems that arose in connection with the project. In fact, the special representatives became figure-heads, and the administration of the project came to rest with the project manager, who was always an expatriate. If he sought advice at all, he sought it from Sweden. Needless to say, this added to the isolation of his organization in the developing country.

As regards Swedish technical assistance, the present trend is in favour of starting the co-operation on the basis of a rather more comprehensive and explicit policy statement, incorporated in an operational plan for the project, while delegating as much power as possible to the executive agency of the receiver country to work on the basis of this policy statement. The main difference between this and the earlier system is that the scope of activities, resource requirements and administrative features of the project are now more carefully elaborated in connection with the basic agreement. Also, organizational solutions are sought, under which the project is from the beginning formally — and later more so in fact — integrated into the receiver's administration (cf. G. Westring, op.cit., p. 283).

40 See, for example, Article 4 of the Agreement on Technical Co-operation between the Government of Denmark and the Government of the Republic of Uganda of July 3, 1968. Article III (2) of the Agreement on Technical Co-operation between Sweden and Kenya of January 23, 1969, states that "in the performance of their duties the personnel made available by SIDA shall be under the exclusive direction of the Kenya Government or the agency corporation or body to which they are assigned". Similar provisions are contained in the development agreements concluded by Norway and Finland.

41 For example, in an Agreement on Technical Co-operation between Finland and Zambia of 1970, Article III (Status and Utilization of Finnish Officers) is by far the longest provision of the Agreement. In the Annex, in which the obligations of the Zambian Government are specified, the benefits to be accorded to all Finnish officers run to such details as "one refrigerator, one deep-freezer, one record-player" and many other things. The Finnish experts are also entitled to import goods into Zambia tax-free. The Swedish agreements go into similar detail, as is amply shown in Annex II to the Agreement between Sweden and Kenya of January 23, 1970, entitled "Obligations in Regard to Personnel made available by SIDA". The status of the experts is the essence of the Agreement on Scientific and Technical Co-operation between the Government of Denmark and the Government of the United Republic of Tanzania of April 5, 1967; the Agreement is actually about nothing else. Similarly, five of the eleven articles of the Agreement on Technical Co-operation between Norway and Tanzania of August 14, 1969, are about the privileges, exemptions and entitlements of experts.

42 For example, the Agreement of Technical Co-operation between Tanzania and Norway of August 14, 1969, distinguishes two categories of personnel. (1) *Experts*, who are the officers whose salaries are fully paid by the NORAD and whose appointments are arranged by the NORAD. They may serve in "an advisory or operational capacity". (2) *Operational personnel* are officers whose salaries are merely subsidized by the NORAD and whose duties are governed by the local contract concluded between them and the Government of Tanzania, which, of course, has to be approved by the NORAD prior to signing. The functional difference between the experts serving in an "operational capacity" and the "operational personnel" is not clear. The Agreement between Sweden and Kenya on Technical Co-operation of January 23, 1969, states expressly that "in the performance of their duties the personnel made available by SIDA shall be under the exclusive direction of the Kenya Government or the agency, corporation or body to which they are assigned". Almost identical is the provision in the Agreement between Finland and Zambia of 1970.

43 The Agreement between Norway and Tanzania of August 14, 1969, states in

Article V (4): "It is intended that each operational officer appointed under this Agreement shall in all respects be a member of the Civil Service of Tanzania and shall be bound by the rules and regulations thereof, so far as they are consistent with the terms of this Agreement."

44 For an excellent comparative study, see Anne Marie Lövgren, *Privileges and Immunities in Bilateral Technical Co-operation Agreements*, Stockholm: University of Stockholm, 1970, 137 pp. (doctoral thesis, mimeographed).

45 For example, under Article VIII of the Agreement on Technical Co-operation between Norway and Tanzania of August 14, 1970, "The Government of Tanzania shall accordingly indemnify and hold harmless officers provided by NORAD against any and all liability suits, actions, demands, damages, costs or fees on account of death, injuries to person or property, or any other losses resulting from or connected with any act performed or omission made in the execution within the territory of Tanzania of projects assisted under the terms of this Agreement, short of acts amounting to reckless misconduct of such officers."

46 In earlier agreements entered into between Sweden and Ethiopia, the experts were granted exemption from the payment of customs charges during their whole period of duty. On Swedish initiative, these exemptions were curtailed in later agreements, and in one of the latest agreements the Swedish experts are granted only "first arrival" exemptions (Lövgren, op.cit., p. 18).

47 From an accountant's point of view this is, of course, quite logical. After all, the country sending the expert pays his salary and fare and, above all, provides the assistance in connection with which the expert is sent to the country. On the face of it, the recipient country certainly gets the expert much more cheaply than if it had to employ him under the overseas recruitment scheme.

For example, in the Agreement on Technical Co-operation with Denmark of July 3, 1968, the Uganda Government not only granted the Danish experts the usual tax and customs-duty exemptions and exemption from legal proceedings in respect of words spoken and written and all acts performed by them in their official capacities but also accepted the obligation to provide the long-term experts with the following facilities, which bear a strong resemblance to a private contract between a firm and an employee rather than a provision in an agreement between two governments:

For each long-term expert provided under this Agreement the Government of the Republic of Uganda shall provide:

(a) Housing with hard furnishing for the expert and his family; housing and furnishings will be of the same standard as that provided for officers of the Government of the Republic of Uganda of comparable status whose terms of appointment specify an entitlement to housing, on payment of subsidized rent. Water, telephone and electricity charges in respect of such housing will be the responsibility of the expert. If the expert initially resides in a hotel, the Government of the Republic of Uganda shall fulfil its obligation by refunding to the expert an amount equivalent to 50 per cent of the full hotel bill (boarding and lodging but excluding any extras, such as laundry, etc.), provided that the rate paid at the hotel is reasonable according to prevailing local rates and that the hotel and particular accommodation therein occupied by the expert are not above the standards which an officer of comparable status might reasonably expect. Subsistence allowance during official journeys will be paid at the same rates as for officers of the Government of the Republic of Uganda;

(*b*) Local support for he work of the expert, including office and/or laboratory space with all the normal facilities thereof, secretarial services and/or laboratory assistance, and free postage and telecommunications for official purposes;

(*c*) Local transport for official journeys of the expert to the same extent as provided for officers of the Government of the Republic of Uganda of comparable status. For official journeys performed by the expert in his personal motor car, mileage allowance will be paid at the same rates as are paid to officers of the Government of the Republic of Uganda;

(*d*) Transport from the point of entry to the duty station on arrival in Uganda and from the duty station to the point of departure at the end of the assignment for the expert, his personal belongings, his family and their personal and household effects;

(*e*) Medical services and facilities for the expert and his family to the same extent as provided for officers of the Government of the Republic of Uganda and their families;

(*f*) The assistance of the Commissioner of Customs and Excise in clearance through customs of the personal and household effects of the expert to the same extent as is provided for technical-assistance personnel of other countries serving in Uganda.

48 The Agreement between Norway and Ghana of July 29, 1968, concerning the Nautical College at Nungua.

49 The Agreement of August 14, 1969, between Norway and Tanzania on Technical Co-operation.

50 They are exempt from personal and income taxes and any other direct taxes, and are immune from civil liability suits, as specified above.

On the other hand (according to article V), these experts have to comply with the same regulations as the Tanzanian personnel (for example, length of vacation etc.). Operational experts are provided by Denmark and Norway but not by Sweden nor Finland. In connection with their status there are some formal questions of interest. For example, in the above-mentioned agreement (note 49) between Norway and Tanzania, there is a provision concerning the recalling of experts (article IV, 2). Such a provision does not exist for the operative personnel. If need be, their services will probably be terminated according to the rules of the Tanzanian Civil Service.

51 The Agreement of 1970 between Finland and Zambia on Technical Co-operation.

52 In the eighth edition of Oppenheim's *International Law* (London: Longmans, 1963, p. 683) H. Lauterpacht refers to a number of cases of treaties entered into by the European States with some Asian and African States, as the result of which their subjects, when they had entered the territory of these Asian and African States, remained wholly under the jurisdiction of their home States.

53 The Convention on the Privileges and Immunities of the United Nations was adopted by the General Assembly of the United Nations on February 13, 1946 (for the text of the Convention, see United Nations Treaty Series (UNTS), vol. 1:15). The Convention on the Privileges and Immunities of the Specialized Agencies was adopted by the General Assembly of the United Nations on November 21, 1947 (for the text of the Convention, see UNTS, vol. 33:362). After their adoption by the General Assembly the conventions were open for accession

by the member states of the United Nations. In 1950 the United Nations Expanded Programme of Technical Assistance was inaugurated. The specialized agencies
also take part in this programme. The assistance mainly consists of the providing of
expert advisers to underdeveloped countries, fellowships and scholarships to
persons from underdeveloped countries, the organizing of seminars and the supply-
ing of equipment (see Kirdar, Uner, *The Structure of United Nations Economic
Aid to Underdeveloped Countries,* The Hague: Nijhoff, 1966, p. 18). Individuals
employed by the United Nations for the purpose of carrying out these programmes
are officials of the United Nations, working to fulfil the purposes of the United
Nations, just as much as the officials stationed at headquarters. They are therefore
granted the same privileges and immunities in the United Nations Standard
Technical Co-operation. In so far as the Convention is applied to the experts, it
means that they enjoy the privileges and immunities not only in the receiving
country but also in all countries which have acceded to the convention.

54 A.M. Lövgren, op.cit., p. 7.

55 The Agreement of June 26, 1964, between the Government of Denmark and the
Government of Kenya on the Establishment of a Women's College in Nairobi.

56 According to Article VIII (2) of the Agreement of November 16, 1970, between
Denmark and Botswana on Technical Co-operation, the Government of Botswana
shall have the right to request the recall of any officer whose work or conduct is
unsatisfactory. Before exercising such right, the Government of Botswana will
consult with the Government of Denmark. Similar provisions are contained in all
agreements on technical co-operation.

57 Cf. the Development Credit Agreement concerning the Grain Storage Project of
July 2, 1970, the procedure is identical with that envisaged in the Development
Credit Agreement between Sweden and Ethiopia of June 3, 1969.

58 Pantheon Books, New York 1970, p. 360.

59 Statistics of flows of "aid" are usually unreliable. This is an area in which politics
reigns supreme and in which the lack of critical appraisal is very detrimental (Otto
Morgenstern, *On the Accuracy of Economic Observations*, Princeton 1963, p.
282). The DAC statistics of "net flows of aid" produced by the systematically
biased DAC secretariat of the OECD is a case in point. For example, year after
petty fascist Portugal is given the place of honour as having the largest "flows" to
underdeveloped countries in comparison with its gross national product (Myrdal,
op.cit., p. 234). The interesting thing about the Swedish statistics is that they are
"calculated on public aid, pure and simple. Private flows are thus not included in
the Swedish calculations of aid" (Myrdal, op.cit., p. 361).

60 S. Lindholm, *U-landsbilden*, Stockholm 1970, p. 238.

61 "Taken together, the main trading partners of South Africa, namely, the United
Kingdom, the United States, France, the Federal Republic of Germany and Japan,
accounted for more than 75 per cent of the total increase in South African exports
between 1962 and 1969. During the same period, these countries alone imported
over 60 per cent of Pretoria's total exports. They constitute the main market for
South African exports and the chief source of supply for its imports, to the extent
that South Africa ranked among the top twelve trading nations of the world in

1968, with exports exceeding 1,500 million rand and imports attaining the high figure of 1,880 million rand"(*Report of the Administrative Secretary-General* [of the Organization of African Unity] *covering the period from February to September 1970,* Addis Ababa, September 1970, para. 91).

ANNEX I

SEVEN POINTS ON SWEDISH FOREIGN AID POLICY

During the 1970's, Swedish foreign aid policy should be expanded into an internationally oriented development policy. It should bring new life into our foreign policy and give a new, global dimension to our political life as a whole. This work should be characterized by the following broad aims.

(1) Public opinion

To awaken and guide public opinion and gradually make the Swedish people aware of the world they live in and the global society that is emerging. This requires that the words and deeds of opinion-makers, and of the government in particular, should consistently treat even traditional domestic issues in an international perspective that does not stop at the frontiers of Scandinavia or Europe. Our industrial policy, our agricultural support system, our social-welfare system, our employment policy, our educational system and so on should be internationalized by judging our actions in relation to the world, not only in relation to ourselves.

(2) Decision-makers

To give domestic decision-makers a more active role in international policy-making and strengthen the agencies within Sweden and on the international level that formulate international policy. Before approving an appropriation

From Ernst Michanek, *The World Development Plan: A Swedish Perspective*, Uppsala 1971, pp. 67-71.
© Ernst Michanek 1971. Reprinted by permission.

of 400 million Swedish crowns (soon to be 800 million or more) for the development programs of the UN and the World Bank, the Swedish Parliament should request detailed reports on the activities of international agencies in the sphere of economic development. Assistance programs should be reviewed both in terms of how the $1 billion annually available to the UN and the World Bank are being used, and in terms of what policy guidelines are being followed. Sweden's role in shaping the policies of these international agencies through governing bodies, committees and assemblies should be summarized in Parliament in such a way as to make Members of Parliament realize their own responsibilities, thereby stimulating them to take a greater interest in these matters.

(3) The developing country

To put the people of the developing country in the centre of development cooperation programs. In the current perspective of starvation, ignorance and oppression, the aim of economic development amounts to nothing less than a social revolution. By giving the people of poorer countries a chance to share in the material and spiritual resources of the world, we are at the same time adding to these resources. Our commitments to developing countries through the UN system and other means should seek, above all, to fulfil the needs and wishes expressed by the poorer nations themselves. Our commitment must be based on an improved knowledge of each country, acquired through close and continuous contact with its people. Our assistance should follow guidelines established by the developing country itself, and drawn up by that country's own political leaders and experts, whose numbers and experience are growing. Only in this way can our contributions to the poorer countries become a part of their own efforts for economic development. In our own planning for development cooperation, we should attempt to make direct use of the expertise available within the developing countries.

(4) The United Nations system

To design our policy towards developing countries and our participation in the UN so that we systematically support, stengthen and complement international efforts in the poorer countries as a whole. We bear a large part of the responsibility for the success of the UN system. On issues connected with disarmament, peace research and mediation of conflicts between states, Sweden has not hesitated to take initiatives and has made contribution of high quality. When it is practicable, we should support, energetically and through actions of our own, the interests of the poorer countries in the utilization of the oceans, outer space and the biosphere as a whole beyond the limits of national frontiers. In a similar fashion, we should experiment with initiatives in trade relations. We should try to give support to the creation and strengthening of regional partnerships between developing countries. We are continuing to work for a better coordinated and more efficient UN development assistance system. One of our goals should be to emphasize more clearly the role of the World Bank as a UN agency for development financing, while preserving the efficiency of the Bank. We should play an active part in expanding the global strategy for economic development that has been presented, making it into a continuing action program for cooperation in many specialized fields.

(5) Concentration

To concentrate our resources on a few key issues and topics and attempt to play a major role in world developments in these fields. The issue of population control should receive the highest priority. The problems of population growth and birth control remain, for the time being, the most pressing of all, yet very little work has actually been done toward solving them. The need for immediate action to protect the human environment is a direct outgrowth of over-population and over-use of resources. This applies both to the most technologically advanced and to the most underdeveloped countries. In problems such as food and water shortages, destruction of natural resources, the over-expansion and decay of urban areas, the crisis in education and the growth of chronic unemployment, we should make our contribution in the form of concerted attacks on limited areas, where our potentials for success are particularly favourable. In 1968, the Swedish Parliament approved a goal of 1% of the GNP for overseas development assistance. If this goal is fulfilled, we will have the financial resources to play an important role in key areas of development work in poorer countries. An estimated 20 billion Swedish crowns ($4 billion) will be available for Swedish assistance to development cooperation during the next decade. Used properly, these funds could yield great results for the world. Sweden is no longer necessarily a small country in matters of international cooperation.

(6) Research

To expand and take full advantage of our resources, in order to place our research facilities at the disposal of international development work. We have the potential (in many areas far from fully exploited) for giving our research activities an international flavor and channeling their results in such a way as to meet the needs of the community of nations. Our research institutions should never be placed in such a position that they have to accept financial support from other countries in order to pursue assignments of international importance. We should take advantage of our opportunities to make independent Swedish research contributions and also to provide support to research in collaboration with developing countries. Among suitable areas of research are contraceptive technology, environmental protection, utilization of natural resources, food production, educational technology and problems of human co-existence and social adjustment.

(7) Cooperation

To find ways to take practical advantage of the skills and resources of all those who wish to participate in development work: young people, national organizations, business corporations, etc. The desire to take part in the practical work of economic development is already greater among certain population groups than in our capacity to absorb their work. The commitment of the younger generation to internationalism is a resource which should be made use of. Our non-profit-making national organizations are also in a position to make larger contributions to development co-operation programs. Business interests in the broadest sense of the term — including cooperative societies, government-owned companies and labor market organizations — have resources which can be put to use in development work without commercial or similar purposes being brought into the foreground. A major task facing the Swedish organizers of development-cooperation programs is to create more opportunities for collaboration with all the various groups who are motivated by a belief in international solidarity. Our goal is to mobilize those wishing to contribute their talents towards a peaceful revolution, whose aim is to increase the resources of mankind and to distribute them more equitably.

ANNEX II

BASIC PLAN FOR SWEDISH OFFICIAL DEVELOPMENT ASSISTANCE, 1969/70 - 1972/73.

Programme	Appropr. 1969/70 million $	Appropr. 1970/71 million $	Min. plan. levels 1971/72-1972/73 million $		Total 1970/71-1973/73 [a] million $
General contributions to multilateral programmes	50.9	54.6	(68.6)	(79.3)	(202.5)
Of which:					
UNDP	18.6	21.1			
UNICEF	2.9	3.9			
UNHCR, UNRWA	0.6	0.8			
IDA	17.0	20.0			
Regional Banks	3.5	0.5			
World Food Programme (incl. FAO)	8.3	8.3			
Bilateral development assistance	67.6	94.6	(110.1)	(129.5)	(334.2)
Of which:					
Credits	27.0	41.5	(48.3)	(58.0)	(147.8)
Grants	40.6	53.1	(61.8)	(71.5)	(186.4)
Unallocated funds, administration, recruitment, training and information	3.9	5.2 [b]	(7.9)	(10.0)	(23.1)
Total	122.5	154.6	186.6	218.8	560.0
Increase from preceding year		32.1	32.0	32.2	

[a] Appropriations for 1970-1, commitments and minimum planning levels for 1971-2 and 1972-3.

[b] This amount has been partly allocated for operational purposes.

Norwegian net official development assistance (in millions of dollars).

	1968	1969
UNDP	4.890	5.245
UNICEF	0.555	0.720
UNRWA	0.091	0.112
UNHCR	0.175	0.269
WFP	2.314	2.365
Other UN agencies	0.022	0.270
Total, UN agencies	8.047	8.981
Other multilateral agencies		
ITC		0.122
FAC (Food Aid Convention)		1.556
Other		0.161
Total, other agencies		1.839
IDA, 1st replenishment	1.111	1.002
IDA, 2nd replenishment	4.402	3.799
Asian Development Bank	0.500	0.500
Total, capital subscription	6.013	5.301
Bilateral projects and technical assistance	4.653	8.380
Nordic projects	0.580	0.537
Emergency food aid	6.163	2.238
Total, bilateral grants	11.396	11.155
OECD consortium to Turkey net	0.497	0.489
Credit to India	0.616	0.490
Loan to Kenya		1.119
Debt-refinancing loan to Ghana		0.151
Total, bilateral loans	1.113	2.249
Grand total	26.569	29.525

Danish development assistance 1962-70 (in millions of dollars).

	1962-3	1963-4	1964-5	1965-6	1966-7	1967-8	1968-9	1969-70
Technical assistance aid								
UN development programme	2.667	2.933	3.733	4.800	6.000	5.733	6.933	10.133
Other multilateral aid		0.067	0.013	0.267	0.453	1.333	1.173	1.747
Bilateral, incl. Nordic projects	0.760	1.333	2.147	3.347	5.333	7.413	10.360	12.320
Financial aid								
Multilateral:								
The World Bank and the International Development Assoc.	2.240	2.560	1.160	2.827	2.080	3.080	0.893	6.667
Regional development banks					0.227	0.227	0.253	0.733
The World Food Programme	0.226	0.800	0.333	0.320	1.533	2.053	3.440	4.000
The Food Aid Convention							1.947	0.920
Bilateral:								
Government loan		0.133	0.800	2.267	4.240	4.667	12.000	9.053
Humanitarian aid								
Multilateral:	0.333	0.307	0.307	0.453	1.000	0.573	0.840	0.893
Bilateral:	0.027	0.080	0.027	0.026	0.040	0.227	0.987	0.053
Various working expenses							0.440	0.667
Denmark's total government aid to the development countries	6.253	8.213	8.520	14.307	20.906	25.306	39.266	47.186

ANNEX V

Flow of Finnish resources to less-developed countries and multilateral agencies (all sums in U.S. $)

	1968 [a]	1969 [a]	1970 [a]	1971 [b]
Total, Official and Private	5,748,583	20,843,217	22,505,732	
Official	2,974,583	9,647,217	6,826,032	12,696,595
Private [c]	2,774,000	11,196,000	15,679,700	
Total, Official bilateral	753,672	1,767,527	1,263,206	5,187,857
Grants, technical assistance	753,672	1,767,527	1,263,206	3,997,380
Loans				1,190,476
Total, Official multilateral	2,220,911	7,879,689	5,562,825	7,508,738
The World Bank Group (IBRD, IDA)		2,720,000	1,359,990	2,380,952
UN Agencies (UNDP, UNIDO, WFP, UNICEF, UNHCR, UNRWA, etc.)	1,718,911	2,446,200	3,136,905	4,915,880
Asian Development Bank	500,000	500,000	500,000	
Others (the 1967 Food Aid Convention, IPPF, ISVS, IRC, etc.)	2,000	2,213,489	565,932	211,905
Private Investment and lending, net	417,000	672,000	879,700	
Private Export credits, net	2,357,000	10,524,000	14,800,000	

[a] Disbursements.
[b] Commitments.
[c] Includes net flows to European recipient countries (Cyprus, Gibraltar, Greece, Malta, Spain, Turkey and Yougoslavia).

ANNEX VI

Organization chart of the Swedish International Development Authority (SIDA).

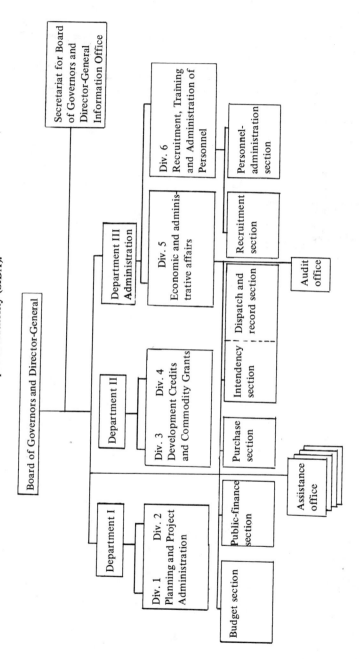

ANNEX VII

Organization chart of the Norwegian Agency for International Development (NORAD).

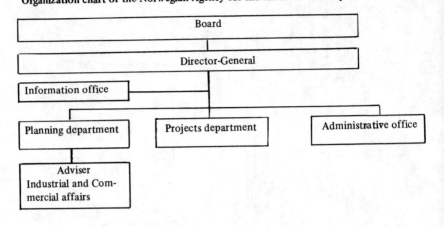